MAYNARD

MAYNARD

History and Life Outdoors

DAVID A. MARK

THE History PRESS

Published by The History Press
Charleston, SC 29403
www.historypress.net

Cover images: Courtesy of the Maynard Historical Society.

First published 2011
Manufactured in the United States
ISBN 978.1.60949.303.5

Library of Congress Cataloging-in-Publication Data

Mark, David A.
Maynard : history and life outdoors / David A. Mark.
p. cm.
Includes bibliographical references.
ISBN 978-1-60949-303-5
1. Maynard (Mass.)--History. 2. Maynard (Mass.)--Social life and customs. 3. Outdoor life--Massachusetts--Maynard--History. 4. Natural history--Massachusetts--Maynard. 5. Maynard (Mass.)--Description and travel. 6. Outdoor recreation--Massachusetts--Maynard.
I. Title.
F74.M46M28 2011
974.4'4--dc23
2011039783

Contents

Preface

An author, speaking to people who yearned to be authors, was asked, "How did you know you wanted to be a writer?" Her reply included how she had once asked a painter how he came to be a painter. He replied, "I liked the smell of paint." Well, I liked words—and facts. I always have.

My parents owned books. I say this because I remember baby-sitting for boys down the street and being astonished that there were no books whatsoever in their house, but there were three color TVs. My growing up in a house filled with books was a way to figure out how adults think.

Much of the content in this book first appeared as a column "Life Outdoors," appearing in Maynard's *Beacon-Villager* newspaper. Brian Nanos, who was the editor at the time, was kind enough to let me start. Bruce Coulter, who succeeded Brian, was kind enough to allow me to continue. Both of them welcomed photos to accompany the articles, which resulted in many of the photos used in this book.

Jean D'Amico, my wife, always read my work before it was submitted to the newspaper and again in manuscript form. Her comments—"too many facts, this is confusing, jumped the shark here"—were always helpful. Louis D'Amico, Jean's brother, drew the water bottles image. Felice Katz, an illustrator, created the two graphs. The Maynard Historical Society loaned use of photos, as did Dave Griffin, William Leonard Jr., John O'Buck and Lisa Bailey. All other photos were taken by me. Commissioning Editor Jeff Saraceno, Project Editor Amber Allen and unnamed image editors at The History Press took those scattered bodies of words and images and helped shape them into this book. All these contributions are deeply appreciated.

This book is dedicated to my parents, Joseph and Stella Mark; my siblings, Charles, Joshua and Suzanne; their families; my wife; and our children, Rachel and Daniel. Jean and I have been together for many years. When we met, we were stubborn, individualistic people with radically different interests—and still are. I relish the differences. Some children cling to their parents when it is time to take first steps, favoring the known to the unknown. From her beginnings, Rachel pursued the unknown. She is living an exciting life on the West Coast. Her path continues to unfold. Daniel left this world at the age of twenty-five. From birth, he struggled to overcome the handicaps associated with mental retardation, cerebral palsy and epilepsy. He had achieved his goals of semi-independent living away from his family, had jobs, had friends and had the love of many people. He is deeply missed.

Chapter 1

Maynard

Why "Outdoors"

Always a Mill Town

The clichéd image of a New England farm village centers on a town green framed by churches, a cemetery, a town hall, perhaps a library and a meeting hall. The rest of the village was a collection of scattered farms, maybe a small mill or inn. Some people did not see their neighbors from week to week except at church services.

Mill towns on the other hand were dominated by huge brick buildings, plus a railroad station, boardinghouses, taverns and stores. Streets were short, house lots small, and many people—women and children included—walked to work at the mill in the morning, walked home for lunch, then back to the mill for the afternoon shift.

Maynard's beginnings were akin to a fast-growing tumor on the bodies of farm-based Sudbury and Stow. True, these villages had their businessmen operating saw- or gristmills, inns and blacksmith shops, but there was a striking difference between those operations employing family, plus an apprentice or a couple of indentured servants, versus the immigrant-absorbing maw of the American Industrial Revolution, circa 1820 to 1870. Growth was so rapid that by the time Maynard seceded from Sudbury and Stow in 1871, this cluster of businesses and housing informally known as Assabet Village had a larger population than either of its parents.

Mill towns go through boom and bust cycles. Maynard was no exception, logging in at five busts. The woolen mill operations that dominated the

The mill complex from Sudbury Street in 1900, across a frozen mill pond. Note the train on the siding in front of the building on the left. In 1916, the pond was temporarily drained and partially filled in to create land for two more buildings. Where the tracks were became the road running under the parking garage and through the middle of what is now Clock Tower Place.

town for over one hundred years began in 1847 under Amory Maynard and William Knight in a modest-sized complex of wood-framed buildings. The mill failed in 1857. It was resurrected in 1862 under Goddard, Browne and Maynard to meet U.S. Army demands for blankets and other woolen goods for the Civil War. In 1898, the mill complex, operating under the name Assabet Manufacturing Company, failed again, this time costing many of the employees their savings in addition to their jobs. Anger was so high in town that the people considered changing the name back to Assabet Village.

A year later, the American Woolen Company, a huge multistate operation, bought the mill on the cheap, added more buildings and electricity and reopened in 1902. Over time, the mill complex added more buildings.

The Great Depression closed the mill in 1931. There was one last hurrah, as woolen mill operations restarted during World War II, then limping on until 1950. After the final closing as a mill, Maynard was quiet to the point that kids could play hopscotch on Main Street.

The next boom/bust was the rise and fall of the house of DEC. Digital Equipment Corporation started renting a small bit of space in the mill complex in 1957 to produce minicomputers, an exciting innovation compared to IBM's mainframes. With Maynard as its world headquarters, DEC took over the mill complex by 1974. DEC maxed at over 100,000 employees worldwide, with annual sales exceeding $10 billion. DEC had its own heliport in Maynard, with frequent flights to and from Logan airport. But by 1990, the company was less than 10 percent of what it had been, sold what was left to Compaq, then folded its tents in Maynard, leaving the mill complex nearly empty again.

The most recent boom cycle started in 1998 with new buyers and a town-voted, fifteen-year Tax Increment Finance Agreement. By 2000, the complex, now called Clock Tower Place, after the town's signature clock tower built by Lorenzo Maynard in 1892, was filled to capacity again with a mix of companies, including Monster.com and Powell Flutes. One realized consequence was a revitalized downtown, with over fifty businesses and eating establishments.

The recession of 2008–2011 led to some rental vacancies in the mill complex. Maynard also evidenced business vacancies. As the economy recovers, these are expected to fill again. Against this, the tax advantage is winding down, meaning that Clock Tower Place will no longer be able to offer rent rates at an advantage to other office complexes in the Routes 128 and 495 region. But being in the middle of a functioning town offers social amenities that an office complex off in the fringes, surrounded by a parking lot desert, cannot match.

The temporary trestle and pipe, which was constructed in 1916 to convey water across the drained mill pond to the mill's powerhouse while the new buildings were being built.

WHY "LIFE OUTDOORS"

This collection mixes local history, observations on nature and outdoor recreational activities as a means of exploring what Maynard offers to anyone willing to move away from too much time looking at electronic screens and not enough time spent seeing, hearing, touching and smelling the life going on outside. Looking harder—looking with an informed eye—finds stories on the edges of history and in the subtler nuances of nature. The questions start simple: Where did all of Maynard's stone walls go? Why are the coyotes so much bigger than what I saw in the Southwest? Was that really a "hundred year" flood? What are those old posts sticking up out of the pond? The answers always hold surprises.

Mixing history with nature and recreational activities does not initially make sense, but it does. The nature we have in eastern Massachusetts is not synonymous with "wild." The woods on Summer Hill were not always woods. In fact, none of the woods anywhere near here are original growth, perhaps with the exception of a ravine or two on the side of Mount

Almost one hundred years later, remnant posts of the trestle still stand above the water level of the refilled pond.

"Indian Clubs" were a popular exercise apparatus circa 1900. Schoolteachers would lead their students in exercise routines using three-fourths pound clubs, while "manly men" would be coached at the YMCA in the use of three-, four- and even five-pound clubs.

Wachusett, and even there nonnative species have intruded. "Not from here" includes honeybees and earthworms, starlings and swans, bittersweet vines and feral cats.

Recreation is also part of history. No colonial-era farm husband or wife could begin to understand the concept of exercise for exercise's sake. But by the middle of the American Industrial Revolution, about the time Maynard came to be, there were enough professions not requiring physical activity that their practitioners began to seek out ways to achieve "Muscular Christianity": the concept of a sound body complementing a sound mind and a saved soul. Gymnasiums and health spas appeared. The invention of inflatable rubber tires led to a golden age of bicycling, a logical demand for improved road surfaces and an unexpected impact on women's overly restrictive clothing and the suffragette movement.

Chapter 2

Eighteenth Century

Maynard, as such, did not yet exist. Farmers continued to settle northern Sudbury and Stow. Very early on the morning of April 19, 1775, Stow's militia mustered on the green and began the long march to Concord, across what is now Maynard, to be part of the battle that began the Revolutionary War. A stone monument commemorating the march stands at the intersection of Concord Road and Route 27.

Whatever Happened to Maynard's Stone Walls?

New England's famed stonework is a reminder of a period 150 to 250 years ago when dry-laid stone was part of every household: fences, walls, foundations, root cellars and more. But anyone who has bicycled through Maynard and neighboring towns will notice Maynard's relative dearth of stone fences and stone walls. Where did the stones go?

It helps to know that during the colonial era, stone was the last choice of materials for fencing fields. Farming through the 1600s consisted of laborious clearing of small fields for vegetables, corn and livestock feed. These plots were bordered by cut brush and branches. The fields were stump filled and worked by hand. As the brush fences rotted, they were replaced by fences made of logs laid horizontally so the ends would overlap as the fence zigzagged along the edge of a field. The goal always was to keep livestock out of the fields. Later still, the stumps of trees cut to clear the fields were

This massive retaining wall behind Maplebrook Park was built in 1847 to support railroad tracks. Trains operated from 1847 to the 1960s. The old railroad right-of-way is the future Assabet River Rail Trail.

rotten enough to pull out of the soil and were laid along the edge of a field. As stones emerged through the eroding soil, they were added to the fences. Stump fences were functional but not handsome, hence the old-time insult "ugly as a stump fence." When the stumps rotted away, post and rail fences were built over the growing rows of stones.

By the end of the Revolutionary War, most of eastern Massachusetts was almost denuded of trees. What wood was left was used for building materials, heat and cooking fires. Stone fencing tall and strong enough to contain cattle took a day's work from two men equipped with an oxcart to gather stone and build ten to twenty feet of a fence. Most of what we see crisscrossing New England was post and rail over stone and laid down between 1775 and 1850. Barbed wire, the easy solution, was not perfected until 1874.

Compared to the surrounding towns of Stow, Acton, Concord and Sudbury, Maynard has very few remaining stone fences. As farms were divided into lots for houses and stone-bordered roads widened, many of the stones were hauled away to build the foundations of new houses.

For example, the houses on Maple Street were built in the 1870s with fieldstone foundations capped by brick above ground. But some remnants of stone fences can be found in Maynard. The hiking trail from Summer Street to the top of Summer Hill crosses a stone fence about halfway up, confirming that the top of Summer Hill was once a near treeless cow pasture. Extensive stone fences can also be seen along the south side of Track Road, the old railroad right-of-way and future Assabet River Rail Trail, as one walks from Maynard into Stow. The woods south of one of these fences is all pine trees approximately sixty years old, suggesting that this pasture was abandoned when the land was seized by the U.S. Army during World War II.

Stone walls are rarer. Stone walls are what we see around churchyards, cemeteries and facing the road in front of the well-off homesteads. In Maynard there are examples of these as mill races, river walls and walls keeping private yards from washing away onto the sidewalks or streets. A large retaining wall holds up the railroad right-of-way behind the apartment building at Nason and Summer Streets. Flat-topped capstones line the tops of low stone retaining walls throughout town. In contrast, copestones were set on the edge on tops of walls to prevent wall sitters. Look for copestones near Maynard's older churches.

SLAVES, INDENTURED SERVANTS AND CONVICTS

Anyone with enough money to pay for transportation to the New World had no intention of working for someone else. The resulting dire labor shortage led to interesting consequences.

Slavery was the law of the land in the Massachusetts Bay Colony from 1641 to 1783, making it the first colony to legally recognize slavery and the first state to end it. Indians captured in various colonist-Indian wars were often shipped to the West Indies to be enslaved there in return for African-born slaves shipped back. A 1754 slave census counted 2,720 slaves ages sixteen and older, with perhaps an equal number of free blacks; this total came to roughly 2 percent of the population but closer to 10 percent for the city of Boston. Wealthy and well-off families, including those headed by ministers, doctors and lawyers, might own one to two slaves.

Historical records of Sudbury and Concord confirm slave ownership: the 1754 census reported fourteen and fifteen adult slaves, respectively. Acton reported one slave; Stow, none.

Although the census recorded no slaves in Stow, there is mention in an 1891 book, *Boxborough: A New England Town and Its People*, of Phineas Taylor owning a slave maid-servant he named Cate. The Taylor-Burroughs land now in Boxborough was part of Stow until 1783. Cate may have been too young to count in the census, as her freedom papers dated April 6, 1772, stated that she was thirty years old when freed. Cate's granddaughter, Mrs. Mary Ann Willis, had in her possession her grandmother's freedom papers at the time the 1891 book was written.

Indentured servants made up a much larger fraction of post-Puritan immigration, perhaps as much as half of the European population arriving in the mid-Atlantic and northern colonies between 1660 and 1760 and definitely more than half in the southern colonies. Agents of English shipping companies scoured England, Scotland, Ireland and Germany to entice young single men and women to, in effect, temporarily enslave themselves for periods of four to seven years in return for free transportation to the New World.

The Atlantic crossing was dangerous. Estimates are that one in twenty-five died en route and then more from disease and hardship after they arrived. Runaways were returned to their masters for a whipping and the addition of one week's servitude for every day escaped. Part of the temptation to signing an indenture contract was that at the end of their service they would receive money, plus twenty-five to fifty acres of farm land. Yet many sold the land and took up paid work in the towns and cities or even went back to Europe.

The third disadvantaged group to reach these shores was convicts. Great Britain's Transportation Act of 1718 confirmed the right to ship convicts to the colonies—including the Caribbean island colonies—and forbade shipping any of them back. Estimates are fifty thousand transported in shackled confinement conditions nearly as bad as the slave trade. Those that survived were indentured for seven years if they had committed minor crimes, fourteen years for major crimes.

Benjamin Franklin wrote against the practice in 1751. England's position was that these felons would become law-abiding citizens in the colonies. He sarcastically suggested shipping America's rattlesnakes to England with the same expectation. Only with the advent of the Revolutionary War did transport to America cease. But within a few years Great Britain found somewhere else to export its convicts and malcontents: Australia.

Once past the 1630–1640 Great Migration of the Puritans, many of New England's immigrants for the next one hundred years were slaves, indentured servants and convicts. Imagine being the only slave living in

Acton, an eighteen-year-old indentured servant loaned to another farmer in return for use of a horse, or a man transported to the colonies for stealing a loaf of bread for his children. Not everyone's genealogy traces to the *Mayflower*.

A SLAVE IN STOW

The previous section only mentioned in passing the story of Cate. What happened to her?

First, her name: Some of the transcribed historic documents had it as "Gate Taylor," others as "Cate Taylor" and one as "Kate," but "Cate" appears to be correct. Second, she probably would not have had "Taylor" as a last name. The man who bought her, Captain Phineas Taylor (1716–1790), was the son of John Taylor, who had arrived in Stow in the late 1600s. "Captain" was an army title. According to Cate's family oral history, as recounted in 1891, Taylor bought her as a very young child in Boston in trade for a box of butter. Taylor chose the name "Cate." In *Black Walden, Slavery and Its Aftermath in Concord, Massachusetts*, a history of the lives of slaves and ex-slaves in Concord, author Elise Lemire notes that slave owners often renamed slaves after purchasing them. Cate was set free at the age of thirty in 1772. The manumission document, described as being in the possession of her granddaughter 120 years later, read as follows:

> *Know all men by these Presents that I, Phineas Taylor of Stow, in the County of Middlesex in the Province of the Massachusetts Bay in New England, Gentlemen, have given and granted, and by these Present Gentlemen, unto my negro maid Servant named Cate, her freedom from me and my heirs and assigns forever. The above said, Cate's freedom is to commence or begin on Tuesday the seventh day of April, 1772, and at the end of the thirtieth year of her age and for the true performance of what is above written, I, the Said Phineas Taylor have hereunto set to my hand and seal this sixth day of April, 1772, and in the Twelfth year of his majesty's Reign George the third King Signed Sealed and Delivered in Presence of Us.*

Cate married Prince Chester on April 23, 1772, just weeks after being freed. Chester was a free man, but had been a slave belonging to army captain Samuel Stone of Lexington. According to Barbara Tornstrom, a Boxborough resident who has deeply researched Cate's history, Stone died in

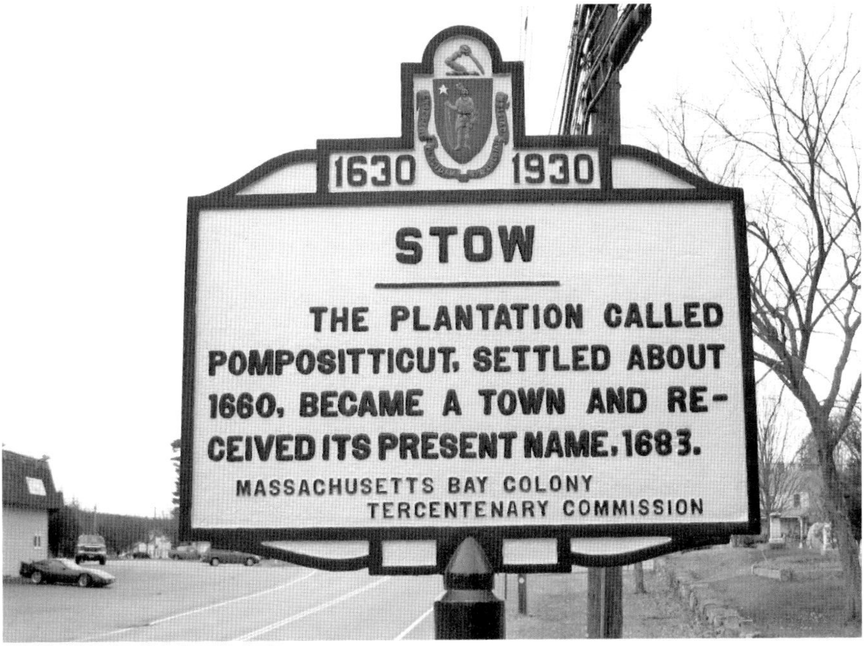

Parts of the original land area of Stow were lost to the creation of Harvard, Lancaster, Groton, Shirley, Boxborough, Hudson and Maynard.

1769. A Lexington history notes that Stone's great-grandfather had arrived in 1635, and that the family was very wealthy, but it had no details on Prince Chester. In passing, it mentions that more than forty people had been owned as slaves in Lexington. Tornstrom speculates that Stone arranged for Prince Chester's freedom either before or upon his death.

Captain Taylor gave the Chester couple a farm in Stow. This area was in Stow until 1783, becoming part of the newly incorporated Boxborough after that. The Chesters' seven children and some of their grandchildren continued to live in the area. Son Prince James Chester married Irenia Cooley, and they had nine children, among them a daughter, Mary Ann, who married a Willis and moved to Groton. Mary Ann Willis was the one with the freedom document, its fate unknown now. Other Chester descendents continued to live in Boxborough, where there is a Chester Road and Chester tombstones in the north cemetery.

Following another descendent, Cate's daughter, Lucy Chester (1774–1849), never married, but when she was twenty-two years old she had a daughter she named Lucy Whitney. The Whitneys were a well-off and numerous Stow

While the burial places of Cate and Prince Chester, freed slaves, are not known, two of their children, Lucy Chester and Prince James Chester, were buried in Boxborough's North Cemetery.

family. An online Whitney family genealogy acknowledges that an unnamed Whitney was probably Lucy Whitney's father. Lucy Whitney (1797–1874) lived her entire life in Boxborough. She married Tower Hazzard. Their son, Tower Hazzard Jr., married Catherine Freeman of Gardner. Their daughter, Martha Ann Hazzard married Allen Hazard of Woodstock, Vermont. The last names are not a coincidence: they were both great-grandchildren of Thomas Hazard, a veteran of the Revolutionary War. Four Hazard men volunteered to serve in the Fifty-fourth Massachusetts Volunteer Infantry Regiment during the Civil War. Hazard descendents today live in Vermont and Massachusetts.

There are also Chester descendents living in Massachusetts. Chester and Hazard families have reunited and are familiar with the family genealogy back to Thomas and Elizabeth Hazard, and Prince and Cate Chester. They are aware that the Taylor-Burroughs farmhouse where their ancestor had been a slave still stands, although the Taylors are long gone. What they don't know—can never know—is what happened to the parents whose daughter was traded away for groceries, 260 years ago.

Chapter 3

Birds and Bugs

In response to an outburst about U.S. golf courses being overrun by Canada geese and/or wild turkeys, a visiting European friend said, "Why don't you just eat them?" We don't anymore—well, not as much—and that has led to a resurgence of these large birds. Likewise, tolerating too many deer has led to a plague of deer ticks and Lyme disease.

Robins in Winter

Robins don't leave anymore. American robins are omnivores, consuming fruit, berries, earthworms and insects. They used to leave—their Latinate name *Turdus migratorius* says exactly that—and then come back in the spring. (The "*Turdus*" part refers to being of the thrush family.) Emily Dickinson's poem "I Dreaded That First Robin So" started with robins and went on to list other spring signs she dreaded such as daffodils and bees. They actually still do leave, but enough stay to make robin sightings year-round not particularly newsworthy. The reasons for seeing robins all year is probably partly due to global warming and to a better winter food supply.

Robins that leave New England spend the winter months in the southern states along the Gulf of Mexico or in central Mexico. Coming back, the males show up first. They travel fifty to two hundred miles a day, staying behind the northward advancing line of temperatures above thirty-seven degrees. That temperature is when earthworms will still appear on the

One robin of a winter flock, sitting in a snow-covered winterberry bush.

surface and also when the ground softens enough for female robins to grab mud with their beaks for nest building. Spring sightings here in New England are a combination of flocks stopping off temporarily but heading farther north and those that have stopped here, declared territories (the males) and started nest building (the females). If you hear a robin singing, it is a local male declaring his territory.

The robins that don't leave, more males than females, gather in flocks of twenty to fifty, sometimes comingling with wintering flocks of starlings. These are not the plump and gentle birds of summer with the hop-hop-hop-stop method of working a lawn for worms and grubs. In winter, robins are noisy and combative, working their way though berry bushes with the aggressiveness of Bostonians at a Filene's Basement sale. They like winterberries but will eat just about any type of berry or fruit. One reason they may find New England more winter friendly now, compared to years ago, is the prevalence of the invasive species Oriental bittersweet and multiflora rose. Both the tree-topping vines and the arching ground brambles are lush with red berries by mid-November.

And why the name "robin"? When the English colonists started arriving in the 1630s, they named the local bird "robin" because its appearance reminded them of the European robin. The species are not related. The European bird is smaller and has a red/orange face and bib with a whitish belly. It is the national bird of the United Kingdom. When the English got to Australia, the local red-breasted birds also became robins. "Flame robins" look a bit like our birds, only brighter.

There was another Atlantic Ocean crossing important to American robins. The common earthworms we see robins tugging from the earth and feeding to their chicks came over with the colonists. Although there were many species of worms native to the Americas, these immigrants are more adept at managing the colder climate of the northeast. Back across the ocean, earthworms are being threatened by another invasive species: the New Zealand flatworm. In parts of Scotland and Ireland, earthworms are now scarce—and the fertility of the soil is declining.

Big Birds

Big Bird of Sesame Street is eight feet, two inches tall, weight and species unknown. History does not record whether Big Bird was ever sighted in Maynard, but our town is home to a number of larger bird species worth getting to know. Each of these exceeds five pounds at its adult weight and has a wingspan of five feet or more.

Canada geese: Males and females can both top ten pounds and generate one pound of goose droppings every day. Once upon a time, Canada geese did not reside in Massachusetts. Breeding grounds were to the far north, wintering grounds to the far south, and we were a flyover state. Over time, and for complex reasons, geese came to live in Massachusetts. Sure, they fly around in low-altitude V formations, but they are not going anywhere distant. In winter, when local ponds and lakes freeze over, our geese move down to the shore to be near open water. But in the spring they return to the same body of water they lived in last year.

Herons: Early risers know that in summer's dawn hours, a great blue heron walks the Assabet River as if it's a personal breakfast buffet. On the menu: fish, frogs and crayfish. Great blue herons nest in colonies but hunt alone. When they find a productive feeding area, they will return day after day—pretty if a nearby river but harsh if it is your goldfish pond. Males and females are similarly colored and take turns on the nest, where they try to raise two to six chicks each summer. Less than one-third make it through the first year. This leggy bird can live ten to fifteen years, spending the warmer months across the United States and southern Canada, then migrating to Central America for the winter. Note: while fish are a first choice, herons are not beyond yakking down baby ducklings or dry-land hunting for snakes, field mice, chipmunks and whatever else will fit down their expandable throat. A YouTube search on "heron eats" will bring up incredible images.

Turkey vultures: These red-headed carrion scavengers find their food by smelling traces of decomposition wafting into the air. New England's vultures raise one to two chicks per year and live more than ten years. They migrate south for the winter. North America's vulture populations are not endangered, but halfway around the world the vulture population of India has been reduced by more than 95 percent over the past fifteen years. Veterinarians began prescribing diclofenac, an anti-inflammatory, antifever drug for milk cows. Traditionally, dead animals are moved to the edge of

Great blue heron with catfish, and yes, that fish went down that throat.

villages and towns to places where vultures congregate. The vultures provide a fast means of cleaning carcasses down to the bones, which are sun dried and sold. But diclofenac is highly toxic to vultures, causing irreversible kidney failure. The drug has been banned since 2006, but illegal import persists. Without enough vultures to eat the carcasses, feral dogs are undergoing a population explosion. India already had twenty thousand deaths per year from rabies. Now that number is growing.

Wild turkeys: These impressive birds were hunted to local extinction by 1850 and not successfully reintroduced to Massachusetts until the late 1900s. Current estimates are that twenty thousand wild turkeys reside in our state. Adult males can easily exceed fifteen pounds, females reach ten pounds. Early mortality is high, but turkeys that make it through the first winter can expect to live five to ten years. Wild turkeys can fly, and sleep perched in trees. Prior to 2011, a flock was often sighted in the early morning at the north end of Acton Street. They've been absent this year, perhaps a consequence of coyotes, which are also being blamed for cat disappearances.

While "flock" is the generic term for groups of birds, each of these species has their own unique group names. Geese are gaggles on the ground and skeins when flying. Vultures make up a kettle while flying but a wake or committee when on the ground. More pluralities include a rafter of turkeys and a siege of herons.

Swans on the Assabet

Mute swans nest each year on the north bank of the Assabet River and have been doing so for years. The swans are often in sight to anyone walking or bicycling on Track Road, the future Assabet River Rail Trail, on the south side of the Assabet River

Swans are long lived and return to the same place to nest. Of the five to eight eggs laid each spring, perhaps one to three cygnets will reach maturity. Unlike Canada geese, parent mute swans do not allow the yearlings to return to the same area the next spring, so the local population is always the parenting pair, plus the new cygnets. Hatchlings start off gray in color, not turning white until their second year. They can paddle about within days after hatching but need sixty days to mature enough to be able to fly.

In flight, these swans make Canada geese look small and slow. Low-flying geese meander about at twenty to thirty miles per hour. Higher-flying geese, the ones actually migrating, are at flock speed thirty-five to forty five miles per hour. In contrast, once swans have powered up to speed, they are doing fifty to fifty-five miles per hour. At more than twice the weight of a ten-pound goose and with a wingspan of seven to eight feet, this is one big bird. The wings of mute swans in flight make a distinctive whooshing sound that on still mornings can be heard more than a half mile away.

Mute swans in the United States do not migrate. Come winter, they shift to the ocean shore, where they may congregate in groups. Come spring, the existing pairs head back to their nesting waters, while the three- to four-year-olds will be pairing up before seeking nesting waters of their own. Swans will often stay in mated pairs for many years, but if one dies, the other will remate. And they are not actually "mute," as they can hiss, snort, yip and so on; it's just they're not being as loud as whooper or trumpeter swans.

Boaters of any type should not approach mute swans. These birds are seriously territorial. On land or on the water, males act to prevent any animal or human from getting near the nest. That yard-long neck may look like a cute sock puppet, but it is wielded more like a poking, pinching hand, combined with hard blows from the forward edge of the wings. Swans have been known to attack dogs, children, swimmers, canoers and kayakers. Swans can sink jet skis, flip ATVs and down ultralight aircraft. OK, maybe not those last three—but really, leave nesting swans alone.

Mute swans are not native to North America and, in fact, are viewed as an invasive and destructive species because of their voracious appetite for aquatic vegetation and harassment of other water bird species. Escaped swans initially established feral populations along the Hudson River, Long Island Sound and Chesapeake Bay but have since spread to the Midwest and Northwest regions, numbering in the tens of thousands and increasing by more than 10 percent a year. Various state programs attempt to control local populations.

"But they are really pretty." Yes, they are. Swans were imported from England starting in the 1800s as living ornaments for private and public garden ponds. The Swan Boats in Boston Public Garden are modeled on mute swans, right down to the orange beak and half-raised wings. Swimming, mute swans hold their heads curved down a bit rather than looking straight forward. Mated pairs often face each other in the water, so in silhouette their necks and heads make a heart shape. The website www.savethemuteswans.com takes the position that mute swans are in fact native to North America and thus deserve the same protections as native birds. The English also exported mute swans to Australia, the natural home of black swans. The two species do not mate.

Worms, Slugs, Snails

Earthworms are such an integral part of New England that it comes as a shock to learn that these worms are an invasive species. Colonial-era gardeners brought lilacs and other plants across the Atlantic, with earthworms as inadvertent passengers in the root balls. The transition from preworm to postworm ecology can be visited in the upper Midwest, where the slow-motion invasion continues to spread. On the preworm side, decaying plant matter creates a "duff" several inches thick on the ground—an ideal habitat for myriad small animal species and also for plant seedlings. On the worm side, leaf litter is at a minimum, and the surface is quite barren.

Charles Darwin's last scientific book, *The Formation of Vegetable Mould through the Action of Worms with Observations on Their Habits*, captured his conclusions from decades of watching earthworms. By discharging their castings on the surface, worms progressively bury whatever lays on the surface under a thickening layer of topsoil. Darwin reported that a layer of sand or cinder on the surface of a field would in five years' time be an inch below the surface, and ten years later, three inches. Flagstone paths, artifacts dropped on a battlefield—everything gets buried. In winter, earthworms migrate downward to stay ahead of soil freeze up. In spring, worms return to the surface when air temperatures reach thirty-five to forty degrees. This timing is matched by migrating robins moving northward from their winter migration to the Gulf of Mexico, in time to mate and start feeding a family.

"Worm charming" refers to tapping, vibrating or pounding the earth's surface as a means to cause worms to rise to the surface. At a mulch pile or other worm-rich environment, jab a pitchfork into the soil and tap the shaft rapidly with a stick. Within seconds, worms will appear. Worm charming videos can be found on YouTube. The best scientific guess is that vibrations mimic sounds made by the digging of worm-hunting moles. Herring gulls have learned to stomp their webbed feet on grassy surfaces in order to feed on worms. (Again, there is video).

A rarer local resident, the great grey slug (*Limax maximus*), astounds. Well, maybe not astounds, if one has visited the Pacific Northwest and come across a banana slug—but still, a slug four times longer than our common garden slug is impressive. Like the earthworms, the great grey is also an invasive species from Europe. Coloring can be grey to brown but always with black splotches. Hence the common name leopard slug.

Garden snails (*Helix aspersa*), another European immigrant, are not the same species as what we dine on as escargot. Worms eat decaying organic materials, whereas slugs and snails will go for the green stuff, making the latter pair the bane of gardeners. Snails live for two to five years, not quite as long as worms but longer than slugs.

These worms, slugs and snails are all hermaphrodites, i.e., have both male and female reproductive organs. Each act of sexual congress has both partners impregnating and both ending up pregnant. Worms manage this in about an hour; slugs, hours; and snails, as long as a day. Of the species mentioned in this article, great grey slugs have the most interesting mating habit. After several hours of intertwining, the two slugs will suspend themselves in midair by dangling from a strand of stringy mucus, spending several more hours mating. Male sexual organs emerge from openings just behind the head and also intertwine. Sir David Attenborough of BBC television did a nice job of explaining exactly what is happening between a pair of leopard slugs. (There is video!).

Eastern box turtles love to eat worms, slugs and snails. Oral history has it that colonists with a slug or snail problem in their root cellar would search the woods for a box turtle to put in the cellar for a month or so. Gardeners without access to a box turtle can consult with their local hardware store staff for more modern means of pest relief.

Deer Ticks and Lyme Disease

Under the "no good deed goes unpunished" trope, a morning stint of volunteer work, clearing invasive plant species in Maynard's woods, resulted in the following: shortly after I sat down at my computer, a small bug stepped out from under the cuff of my sweatshirt and meandered across the back of my hand—an adult deer tick. I brushed the tick into a jar. After starting a work-clothes laundry, conducting a whole body search and taking a shower, I returned to my desk and began to research Lyme disease.

Why "Lyme?" Names can be for symptoms (whooping cough, yellow fever), the discovering doctor's name (Parkinson's, Alzheimer's), a defining population (Legionnaire's disease) or a place (Ebola, Marburg). The villages of Old Lyme and Lyme, in Connecticut, combined population under ten thousand, were the epicenter of recognition of Lyme disease in 1975. The story starts with a mother. Polly Murray had two children diagnosed with juvenile rheumatoid arthritis (JRA). As she commiserated with other parents of children with JRA, she was struck by how common this supposedly rare condition had become in their small community. Murray complained to the

Massachusetts is home to an estimated 100,000 deer. Eastern Massachusetts, between Routes 128 and 495, has 10 to 30 deer per square mile.

state health department, thinking perhaps there was an unknown pollution problem. Her efforts and her list of thirty-nine children with similar symptoms brought in Dr. Snydman of the health department, who brought in rheumatology expert Dr. Allen Steere from Yale University. Dr. Steere made the connection to the possibility of tick-borne bacterial disease. The bacteria responsible for Lyme disease is *Borrelia burgdorferi*. Lyme arthritis, later renamed Lyme disease, could have as easily been Murray's disease or Steere's disease.

A tick's life has three stages played out over two years. Confusingly, people describe deer ticks as the size of a typed period, a poppy seed or an apple seed. All are true. Nearly microscopic uninfected larvae hatch from eggs in late spring, hoping to latch on to a field mouse. One blood meal is all they are after, but if the mouse host is infected, so becomes the tick. The larval tick morphs into the nymph stage and forgoes feeding off animals through fall, winter and early spring. Come May, these poppy seed–sized, possibly infected nymphs are hanging out on ground-level vegetation, hoping for a mouse or bird to brush by. Ground-level gardening work puts humans at risk. Most human infections are from nymphs, contracted May through August. The nymph stage is also one blood meal and done, but if they feed from an infected mouse, this is another vector for infecting the tick. Gorged, they drop off the host to the ground and morph into adults.

Come fall, these adults climb tall grasses and shrubbery with their legs outstretched, hoping to latch onto a passing deer. Once on board, adult females settle in for their third and last blood meal, while males wander around to mate with the females. It helps to visualize each deer as a singles cruise ship. Females overwinter at ground level, and then in the spring, they lay one thousand to three thousand eggs to start the cycle over again. Some adults miss latching on to a deer in the fall, overwinter as adults and are then out in early spring for a last chance at mating and a blood meal. More information is available from the American Lyme Disease Foundation (www.aldf.com).

No deer means no deer ticks, which means no Lyme disease. Extensive land clearing, farming and hunting forced the U.S. white-tailed deer population to under half a million a century ago. The population has long since recovered, and with it, so has the deer tick population. Lyme disease cases in the United States increased from 10,000 in 1992 to 30,000 in 2008. Of that last total, more than two-thirds were in the New England and mid–Atlantic states, with 3,960 in Massachusetts. One could argue that not going into the woods is an answer, but as any gardener, landscaper or farmer in eastern Massachusetts knows, the deer have come to us.

Chapter 4

Bicycling

Massachusetts is small enough to be able to cycle to the next state and back before lunch if you start early enough. Those not wanting to ride alone can join the Nashoba Valley Pedalers or the Charles River Wheelmen.

Riding the Assabet River Rail Trail

In time—perhaps 2016—the Assabet River Rail Trail will be a paved path extending southward from South Acton to the middle of Stow. Years after that, more construction will connect this northern section to the already completed section in Hudson and Marlborough. Meanwhile, volunteers have worked to clear the former railroad right-of-way of downed trees, brush, poison ivy and garbage, so that much of Acton, Maynard and Stow can be biked right now. Maps and pictures are at www.arrtinc.org, but the following is a descriptive tour suitable as a guide for anyone with curiosity, mosquito repellant and good walking shoes.

To go north, start at MapleBrook Park, at the corner of Summer and Maple, in Maynard. The roundtrip distance will be 3.6 miles. The first section was cleared and wood chipped between the rails by ARRT in 2002. North of Cumberland Farms gas station the trail crosses Concord Road and continues behind the auto repair shop. The south end of this section does not drain well after heavy rains, so you may have to backtrack and detour up Acton Road. This half-mile section does not have wood chips covering the railroad ties.

Toward the northern end of Maynard, there is access from the back of the parking lot across from the Massachusetts State Police Forensic Laboratory. There is also access at the northern end just before Acton Street meets Route 27. The trail continues on the north side of Acton Road, and from here on, it can be managed on an off-road bicycle by someone with moderately good bike-handling skills. Cross into Acton, follow the trail north, detour around the front of the Paper Store office complex, reconnect with the Trail by going over a berm and then continue north all the way to Maple Street in Acton. The last half mile requires crossing an old trestle bridge. By midsummer, the Acton section is partially overgrown with grasses and poison ivy, especially north of the trestle bridge. In Acton, there is also easy access from Sylvia Road.

Things to look for on this route are stone posts that once held signs for the train engineers, the Marble Farm historic site, poison ivy, wild grape and bittersweet vines, beaver damage to trees and a hand-operated railroad switch.

To go south, start again at MapleBrook Park. The roundtrip distance will be seven miles. Head down the parking lot behind the Outdoor Store, cross the footbridge and continue on Railroad Street. The white building between the west end of Railroad and Main is at the site of the former train station. Continue on Main, cross Main to go left onto Sudbury (by the ball-shaped, one-time, horse-watering trough) and turn right onto High Street. Partway down High Street on the right is an ARRT sign, marking the beginning of another wood-chipped section. Maynard's Boy Scouts help clear and chip this section. At the far end, turn left on Mill, left again on Route 117, cross Route 117 to continue on Winter Street and make a right at a sign-marked fork onto a dirt road. This is the beginning of Track Road, which goes for nearly three miles into Stow. All of this can be easily managed on an off-road bicycle.

Track Road is a wide dirt road up to Crow Island, then a narrow, and at times wet, path beyond that. The future Rail Trail crosses Sudbury Road in Stow, continues for a short distance, then dead-ends at the unbridged Assabet River. For those with bicycles and ambition, backtrack to Sudbury Road, turn left (west), left again when Sudbury Road veers left and left once more onto Route 62. In about a mile, a sign and parking lot on the right will mark the beginning of the paved portion of the Assabet River Rail Trail, all the way to Marlborough.

Things to look for on this route are the concrete foundation of what used to be the Bent Ice House, Ice House Landing, vernal ponds and skunk cabbage.

"Track Road," part of the future Assabet River Rail Trail, extends from Ice House Landing off Winter Road, in Maynard, miles westward into Stow. Another access is from White Pond Road.

Winter Bicycling

Bicycling with temperatures in the single digits has certain side effects. For example, one's eyes start to tear, and the water evaporates, condenses on the eyelashes and then freezes. Ski goggles solve that problem, but if you want to bring along a water bottle, that also freezes. At temperatures much below zero, nose hairs ice up with each inhale. And your bike very likely no longer shifts gears, so you have to pick one gear before starting out.

The upside to winter bicycling is extending riding into late fall and early spring. Roadies—i.e., the Spandex crowd with the skinny tire bikes—consider Memorial Day to Labor Day as prime riding weather. With the proper clothing, it is possible to start the spring season in March and extend fall riding to at least October, maybe even into November. But once winter sets in, the negatives outweigh the positives: road shoulders are narrowed by snow banks, "black ice" becomes a skidding hazard to someone whose

Dropping the bicycle seat an inch or two for winter riding makes it easier to get a foot down when icy skids inevitably start.

contact with earth is limited to a few square inches of slick tire, plus sand and salt chew up the gears and chain of that $1,500 bicycle. So, it's time to roll out the mountain bike.

The adage for outdoor activities is "There is no such thing as bad weather, only the wrong clothes." Or for the obliviously optimistic, "There is no such thing as bad weather, only different kinds of good weather," by John Ruskin. The list of wrong clothes starts with cotton. Layers are needed, with a layer underneath to wick sweat away from the body and an outer layer that will allow some air exchange without letting the wind of riding take away too much body heat. Local bike shops such as Ray & Sons carry winter gear specific to cycling. The Outdoor Store also has winter sports clothing.

In Maynard, the Summer Hill trail is too steep once there is snow or ice on the ground, but the trails off of Rockland Avenue or behind the schools offer interesting single-track options. Track Road west of Ice House Landing is wide and flat but can get iffy later in winter because of large puddles and deeply rutted snow, ice and frozen mud left by motor vehicle traffic. Quieter residential streets can be fun on a sunny poststorm morning when everyone is out shoveling or snow blowing their driveways. In Stow, there are great off-road options. The Assabet National Wildlife Refuge has opened up about half of the fifteen miles of trails to bicycling. Access to the north parking lot is from White Pond Road. The Trail Guide available at www.fws.gov/northeast/assabetriver has a good map on the third page. Gardner Hill, also known as the Stow Town Forest, offers challenges, ranging from wide, mostly level trails to a challenging single track. Access is from a parking lot at the end of Bradley Lane.

A few practical points: Drop the seat an inch or two so that it is easier to reach out with a foot when the bike starts to skid, under inflate tires or use studded tires, assume there will be ice under the snow, and finish before it starts to get dark. On snow-covered fire roads and wider trails, try to avoid riding on the tracks left by cross-country skiers; watch out for snowmobiles. If riding solo, let someone know where you will be riding and bring a cellphone—you can walk home from a broken bike but not from a broken leg.

Bicyclists Need Hills

"Grade" is elevation gained over horizontal distance traveled. Ten feet higher for 100 feet traveled is a 10 percent grade. State and county roads rarely exceed a 7 percent grade, but local roads can be steeper. The steepest roads in the world have grades a bit over 30 percent. The famously steep streets in San Francisco are just under 32 percent. In Los Angeles, Fargo Street is closed to traffic once a year so bicyclists can give it a go: at 530 feet in length, you gain 160 feet in elevation at a grade of 32 percent. The Fargo Street ascent takes two to five minutes of weaving back and forth from one side to the other, and some riders have been known to have sure-footed spotters trailing behind to stop them if they fall off the bike and start to slide down the pavement.

Ideally, training hills for bicyclists should be both conveniently close and with light car traffic. Three to six repetitions twice a week can be a useful part of a training regimen. A cyclist can chose to train with no electronic devices whatsoever or have handlebar displays showing grade, current speed, average speed, elapsed time, cadence, heart rate, calories burned and power output. The top-end devices will download to a training program on a personal computer.

Going downhill fast concentrates one's thinking. My personal mantra: "Stay on the bike, stay on the bike, stay on the bike." Personal speed record: fifty-three miles per hour, Vermont, 2004.

Here are local climbs with steep grades and little car traffic:

- Birch Hill (Stow): 0.74 miles; 180 feet climbed; average grade, 4 percent; steepest, 12 percent. Start this climb where Sudbury Road crosses the Assabet River, turn right to climb Whitman Street, then turn right again onto Birch Hill Road. Stop where Birch Hill crests, go back and repeat.
- Summer Hill (Maynard): 0.39 miles; 107 feet climbed; average grade, 5 percent; steepest part, 17 percent. Start after turning from Summer Road onto Howard Road, then turn right onto Abbott Road and right again onto Wilson Circle. Descend and repeat.
- Vose Hill (Maynard): 0.14 miles; 65 feet climbed; average grade, 8 percent; steepest, 13 percent. Start after turning off Route 27 onto Vose Hill Road. Ascend. Descend and repeat.

Why all this hill training? Because Mount Wachusett beckons. This local mountain has a road to the summit. Elevation at the peak is 2,006 feet. The distance from downtown Maynard and back is sixty miles. Maynard's elevation is 165 feet, but because of intervening ups and downs, the actual elevation climbed is 3,120 feet going and 1,280 feet coming back. The climbing gets serious past the center of Sterling. Distance to the summit at this point is twelve miles, and there is still 2,000 feet of the climbing to go. Stretches both before and on the mountain exceed 10 percent grade; two on the mountain exceed 20 percent. As for descending, part way up the mountain the road forks to become a one-way route to ascend and a one-way route to descend. Be prepared to grab a lot of brake on this descent, as it is narrow and rough, and for just under a mile, it averages an 11 percent grade, with sections exceeding 25 percent. Those grades are akin to the road down Mount Washington.

There are tools available for people who like to plan their routes. Google Maps will show directions and distances but not elevations. Topographical maps from the U.S. Geological Survey show where the hills are, but they are no help calculating cumulative elevation climbed. Plus, the Maynard map's last update was 1987! But a software program named Topo USA from DeLorme allows users to plan a route, generate directions and print an elevation chart. By dragging the cursor across the chart while in Profile mode, it shows grade at each point along the way. The program also calculates cumulative elevation gained and distances.

Chapter 5

NINETEENTH CENTURY

The Industrial Revolution arrived in full force, with raw materials and factory goods transported by steam-powered locomotives. Harvesting and selling ice was a huge business.

BIRD'S-EYE VIEW

In 1879, the mappers O.H. Bailey & J.C. Hazen drew and published an aerial view map of Maynard. Originals of the printed map are on file at the Library of Congress and the Norman B. Leventhal Map Center of the Boston Public Library. The Center has more than five hundred aerial view maps on file, including not only Maynard but also South Action and Concord Junction (West Concord). There are no records of aerial view maps ever being made for Stow or Sudbury. Copies of the Maynard map in a range of sizes can be purchased from various online vendors.

From the Library of Congress website:

> *The panoramic map was a popular cartographic form used to depict U.S. and Canadian cities and towns during the late nineteenth and early twentieth centuries. Known also as bird's-eye views, perspective maps, and aero views, panoramic maps are non-photographic representations of cities portrayed as if viewed from above at an oblique angle. Although not generally drawn to scale, they show street patterns, individual buildings, and major landscape features in perspective.*

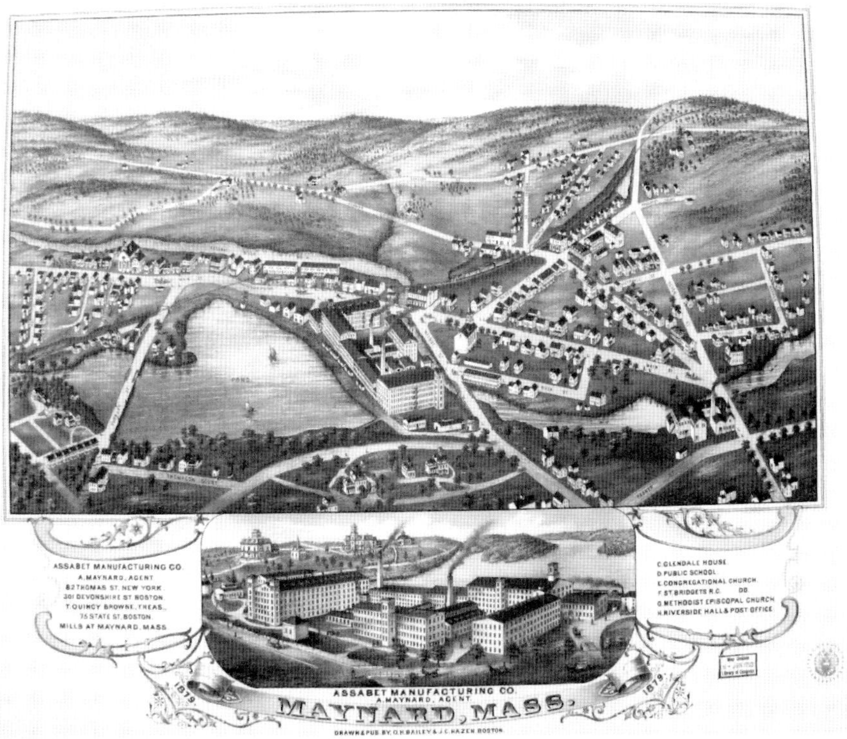

While it is questionable whether sailboats ever navigated the mill pond, there is a tremendous amount of true detail in this etching.

The view of Maynard is as if from a hot air balloon tethered about 2,500 feet straight up from the Glendale Cemetery, facing north. The drawing may not be entirely house-to-house accurate, but major buildings are present and labeled. What is of interest is what was mapped and what is missing. The mill, of course, occupies the center of the map: two smokestacks smoking and a railroad siding between the mill and the pond. The pond is much larger than at present; the mill complex much smaller.

The Maynard mansions—Amory's and Lorenzo's—are drawn in great detail on the hill south of the mill. A large insert below the main map shows the mill in more detail, viewed this time from the north and again with the Maynard mansions in the background. No surprise here, as the map was commissioned by the Assabet Manufacturing Company (AMC), Amory Maynard, agent. AMC went bankrupt twenty years later. Ownership transferred to the American Woolen Company in 1899.

The map shows the major streets—Main, Nason, Summer, Parker, Walnut and Sudbury—and minor streets—Thompson Court, River, Maple, Brooks, Glendale, Pleasant, Percival, Pine, Warren and Summer Lane (now Summer Hill). The Congregational church, eighteen years older than the town of Maynard, is in place. A school stands where the library is now. Saint Bridget's Roman Catholic Church stands on the site of today's police station. A sizeable paper mill with its own power plant was next to the river. Now that site is Tedeschi Food Shop. The Marlboro Branch Railroad crosses right to left, the Assabet River left to right. Glendale House, later renamed the Maynard Hotel, stood at the site of today's Memorial Park, across from the Fine Arts movie theater, until it burned in 1921. There is no Florida Street Bridge over the river or a Mill Street Bridge.

The map may also help roughly date individual houses as being either present by 1879 or built later. For example, Brooks Street shows six houses on the west side—today, eleven—and none on the east. Percival Street shows six close-set, two-family houses exactly where today's Google map shows the same.

Oakley H. Bailey, one of the better-known panoramic artists, lived long enough to see his profession become obsolete. He was born in 1843, served in the Civil War and then took up the panoramic map trade in 1871. He retired at age eighty. The Library of Congress biography cites a 1932 interview in which he said, "Airplane cameras are covering the territory and can put more towns on paper in a day than was possible in months by hand work." He lived until 1947. His life began in the era of kerosene lamps and steam-powered trains and ended in the age of jet planes and computers.

Map vendors include the Boston Public Library at maps.bpl.org, www.imagekind.com, www.wardmaps.com, www.old-maps.com and www.ushistoricalarchive.com. Size options range from as small as eight by ten inches to as large as forty-four by fifty-seven inches.

ICEHOUSES AND THE ICE BUSINESS

"Many years later, as he faced the firing squad, Colonel Aureliano Buendia was to remember that distant afternoon when his father took him to discover ice." Thus begins *One Hundred Years of Solitude*, a fabulistic, multigenerational tale set in the 1800s in a remote village in South America. And if every word were true, that very ice—displayed in a pirate chest by wandering gypsies—could have come from the Assabet River.

In the late eighteenth century, a few wealthy Americans had their own means of having summer ice. George Washington had an ice cellar at Mount Vernon. His letters to his farm foremen exhort them to send slaves to the Potomac River to gather ice. Martha Washington took pride in being able to serve iced punch and ice cream. Boston-based Frederic "the Ice King" Tudor was the first to successfully turn ice into a business. He shipped ice to Havana starting in 1806; he shipped ice to New Orleans; by 1833, he was shipping ice to India! Tudor's business was aided by ice-harvesting inventions developed by his employee, Nathaniel J. Wyeth. Anyone interested in learning more about the ice business should read *The Frozen Water Trade* or *The Ice King*.

Thoreau's *Walden* gives as good a description as any on harvesting ice. As he puts it, a hundred men of "Hyperborean extraction" (later clarified: Irishmen) swooped down on Walden Pond in January 1847. Horse-drawn scrapers moved the covering snow to one side, followed by a horse-drawn ice plow—invented by Wyeth—that made parallel lines two feet apart and four

A Disston Saw catalog from 1918 shows ice saw blades from three to six feet long and priced at one dollar per foot. Handles, sold separately, were one dollar. This was when physical labor paid fifty cents an hour. *Photo by Bill Leonard Jr.*

Large ice tongs were two-handed, but ingenious designs allowed smaller blocks of ice to be managed one-handed. Side by side, these two suggest Grant Wood's *American Gothic*.

to five inches deep. Tremendous handsaws, blades five feet long with a crossways handle at one end, were used to finish the cuts. Loosened foot-thick blocks were floated to shore in a cut channel to be loaded onto sleds and then to railroad cars. A traveling crew of one hundred could manage an acre a day or a bit over one thousand tons of harvested ice. An ice "cake" would measure a foot thick and just under two by four feet. Sawdust would be spread between the stacked cakes to prevent sticking. Thoreau was aware of the India connection, as he writes imaginatively about Walden water mingling with the sacred water of the Ganges.

The Annotated Walden identifies the crew harvesting Walden Pond in the winter of 1847 as under the employ of the firm of Jarvis & Wyeth. This is the same Nathaniel J. Wyeth who built a brick icehouse on the banks of Maynard's Mill Pond in 1849, now Front Street. Later, the Bent family and others owned icehouses upstream of the Ben Smith Dam. The foundation of the Bent Ice House is visible from the path leading east from Ice House Landing. It was positioned so that ice could be loaded from the Assabet River at one end and unloaded onto railroad cars at the other. The symbolic granite blocks at Ice House Landing are two by two by two feet and, hence, not the same dimensions as ice cakes—but easier to sit on.

By the end of the Civil War, most well-off homes in New England cities had an icebox. A cardboard sign put by the window signaled the iceman to make a delivery. Ice sat in a container at the top and there was a drip pipe to a catch pan underneath. Ice was moved with ice tongs. Ice was also being used to chill entire railroad cars in order to deliver unspoiled produce, meat, fish and dairy products. Gloucester fishermen left port with holds full of ice. Demand outstripped supply, and concerns grew about the purity of ice collected from the same waters used for sewage or industrial waste. As early as the 1870s, mechanical means of making ice started to supplant pond ice, but icehouses were still operating on the Assabet into the 1920s. It was not until the advent of Freon coolant in the 1930s that the ice man started to be phased out in favor of the Frigidaire.

Urban Barns

As anyone who has peered down driveways on Maple or Brooks Streets knows there are a number of barns in Maynard that were never part of any farm. These were typically two-story edifices: the first a stable for a horse, plus space for a wagon, the second for hay.

The barn at 10 Maple Street is a good example. The house dates to circa 1870. The barn is a plank-floored twenty-five- by forty-foot structure with modified post and beam construction. The barn was built on a foundation of fieldstones. The rear right side was a horse stall. It is eleven by fourteen feet and has three small windows seven feet up from the floor. The rear left side was a chicken coop. It had nesting boxes for eight hens and a chicken-sized door to the yard. When taking it apart in 2003, evidence was found where rats had gnawed through the floorboards to get to the feed bin. The second floor of the barn has a hayloft door in front and holes above the stall and chicken coop to dump down hay.

While animals are no longer housed in the barn, skunks have on occasion taken up winter residence under the barn. Even when skunks do not spray, there is always an undercurrent of "Oh, yeah, skunk" smell. Neighborhood cats coexist peacefully with the skunks.

This begs the question: "What were these urban barns for?" The railroad came to Maynard in 1849, barely fourteen years after steam locomotives began operating in the United States. Trucks did not make a significant impact on road freight transport until after World War I. So for seventy years, horse-drawn wagons were bringing goods to and from rail yards. The book *Images of America, Maynard, Massachusetts* has many pictures of horse-drawn wagons and carriages, some dating as late as 1926.

The Maynard census of 1871 confirms Maynard as a horse town. As posted in the history section of the town's website, it lists the population for Maynard as 1,820 people in 321 dwellings, plus 275 cows and 79 horses. Maynard's annual town records show the horse population peaking at 256 in 1899. While a few of these horses were carriage horses for the well to do or work horses for farms, many were stabled in urban barns for pulling wagons in and around Maynard. Horses were also stabled at liveries such as Coughlan's Livery, which in addition to boarding horses, sold feed, tack, wagons and carriages. The Fine Arts Theatre stands on the site today.

Clydesdale, Shire and Suffolk were workhorse breeds common at the time. These horses pulled the town fire wagons, delivered milk and picked up garbage. Horses pulled the wagons that delivered ice from the Bent and Comeau Ice Houses on the Assabet River. Laundry wagons would pick up dirty clothes and deliver them back, washed and pressed. Wagons from A. Batley & Sons delivered flowers from the Batley greenhouses on Acton Street. In due time, horse-drawn hearses brought everyone to the cemeteries.

Besides the barns, there are other visible signs of Maynard's one-time horse trade. The Town of Maynard maintained public water troughs for horses. Four still exist in Maynard today and are currently located in front of the Maynard Fire Station, at the intersection of Sudbury and Main, in the traffic island at Concord and Acton Streets and on the lawn of the Boys & Girls Clubs on Route 117. These were donated by Lorenzo Maynard in 1888; Thomas Rafferty, 1894; Warren G. Haynes, 1904; and Asahel Balcom, 1892.

The horse era gradually came to an end after World War I. Although bicycles came into vogue in the 1890s and cars just after the turn of the century, it was the truck industry that had developed during World War I that led to the final decline of urban workhorses. Their urban barns have been recycled to many uses since then.

Old House

Maynard, Brooks, Greer, Hanna, Partridge, Barlow, Marsden, Jones and D'Amico/Mark: those are the families who owned the property at 10 Maple Street from 1870 through the present. A reproduction of an 1875 street map at the Maynard Historical Society shows a house belonging to Charles Brooks, so the house itself is at least 136 years old. As built, the house probably did not have indoor plumbing, but it may have had piped gas for gaslight fixtures. Electric lights did not begin to reach Maynard until 1902, when the mill contracted to provide power for street lights.

Learning the names of the litany of owners—and the price at each sale—required going to Middlesex County Courthouse in Cambridge to leaf through records of property sales. The oldest showed A&L Maynard Company selling the property to Charles Brooks in 1870 for $2,430. Mr. Brooks was fifty-six years old at the time of purchase. The 1870 U.S. census described him as a widower, working at a sawmill, with four teenage daughters.

The deed does not specify whether there was a house on the property at the time of the sale to Brooks, but Amory Maynard and his son, Lorenzo, owned other lots on Maple Street at the time. It is possible they were building and selling houses in addition to owning and operating the mills. In support of this theory, most of the houses on Maple Street and Maple Court have a similar architecture, indicating they were all built at the same time.

The Owners

Before 1870	A&L Maynard Company
1870–1879	Charles G. Brooks
1879–1896	Alexander and Elizabeth Greer
1896–1924	John and Mary Hanna
1924–1926	Charles and Esther Partridge
1926–1953	William and Carrie Barlow
1953–1987	Thomas and Blanche Marsden
1988–2000	Craig and Tresa Jones
2000–Present	David Mark and Jean D'Amico

At first glance that count is nine unrelated owners over 140 years, but a bicycle ride through Maynard's cemeteries complemented what was learned from the deeds. Alexander and Elizabeth Greer bought the house from Brooks in 1879. The 1880 U.S. census listed Alexander as a watchman at

The house dates to at least 1870. More research may require a new sign.

the woolen mill. Alexander and Elizabeth (née Henderson) were both born in Scotland in 1827.

The Greers had three children: Mary, Walter and James. Walter died in 1885 at age twenty-four. James died in 1879 at age sixteen. Mary married John Hanna in 1880. She took over ownership of the house. Thus, two generations of Greers/Hannas owned the house for forty-five years. John was a carpenter at the woolen mill. Mary lived to ninety-one, and in doing so, she survived her parents, brothers, husband and children. The Greer plot is in Glendale Cemetery.

Before she died, Mary Hanna sold the house to Charles and Esther Partridge. Upon Charles's death, it went to their daughter, Carrie Barlow, and, in turn, to her daughter, Blanche Marsden, who had no children. This time, three generations of the family owned the house for sixty-three years. The Partridge/Barlow/Marsden plot is also in Glendale Cemetery. The Marsden inheritors sold it to Craig and Tresa Jones in 1988. Jean D'Amico and David Mark bought the house from the Joneses in 2000.

The house is white with black shutters. The foundation is fieldstone cemented in place, topped with a few feet of brick. The scarcity of stone walls in Maynard suggests that most of the farm walls were recycled into foundations and chimneys. While the stone is likely local, it is very possible that the wood for the wide-plank pine floors, framing and walls was brought in by railroad. Almost all of eastern Massachusetts was denuded of trees by the early 1800s.

Houses change. The Marsdens most likely were responsible for converting a front porch to a room on a concrete slab, extending the kitchen, adding a downstairs bathroom and adding the current back porch with its wooden slat awnings. D'Amico and Mark removed the cramped second-floor bathroom and attic space over the kitchen and converted that into a full-sized bathroom plus a laundry/walk-in closet. As part of this project, the chimney that had once serviced a wood-burning stove in the kitchen was removed.

A Railroad Ran Through It

Noisy, dirty, dangerous: a fair description of what it was like living near a railroad back in the steam era. Steam engines work via external combustion. Rather than diesel being sparked inside the cylinder and explosively pushing the piston away, solid fuel—wood or coal—was used to heat a boiler filled with water. High-pressure steam from the super-heated water was piped to the pistons to provide power. Each exhaust stroke from the piston pushed the depleted steam out the smokestack, mingling with smoke, sparks and cinders from the firebox. External combustion engines are inefficient. Estimates are that only 5 to 8 percent of the heat energy gets converted into horsepower versus 25 percent from diesel. The "chug, chug, chug" sound of a locomotive in movies portraying the steam age is steam from each stroke of the engine's two very large pistons, which were directly linked (no transmission) to the drive wheels.

The fireman's job on a wood-fired locomotive from the 1850s, with its weight 20 to 25 tons, was to keep the fire going and the boiler filled. The tender, behind the engine, would carry about three tons of water and one ton of wood. By the 1870s, most eastern railways had switched to soft coal, and coal remained the fuel of choice until almost the tail end of the steam age in the 1950s. By the end of the steam age, locomotives had become gigantic. An engine could weigh 140 tons, with four small wheels under the front, six very large powered wheels and two smaller wheels supporting the cab at the back, hence a 4–6–2 in engine parlance. The tender could weigh 80 tons with its full load of 30 tons of water and 10 of coal. But nothing this large would have ever run through Maynard.

Back in the 1850s, the fireman threw wood or shoveled coal on the grate in the firebox, which on the older engines was an area of some three by four feet. Ideally, the firebox floor was kept evenly covered several inches deep in red-hot coals. Some 15 percent of wood's weight would be wasted, emerging from the smokestack as fiery sparks and hot cinders. There was less wastage from coal. The fireman also managed water flow from the tender to the engine's boiler, which would generate steam by holding water at 140 pounds per square inch pressure and thus close to 350 degrees Fahrenheit. Low water could result in a catastrophic explosion, while adding cold water too fast could kill steam pressure and thus depower the engine.

The mills in what are now Maynard, Stow, Hudson and Marlborough were serviced by freight trains running on a 12.5-mile-long spur that branched southwest from the Boston-to-Fitchburg line. The branch point was east of what is now the South Acton Train Station. Rails out this way weighed 85 pounds per yard, so a touch over 1,100 pounds per thirty-nine-foot-long rail.

The spur was operative to Hudson by 1850 and extended to Marlborough in 1855. There was also passenger service. A two-car passenger train derailed and tipped over in Maynard on Sunday, April 16, 1911, causing numerous injuries but no fatalities. By that time, the original Fitchburg

The crew stands in front of their 4–4–0 steam locomotive. Four small wheels (two per side) supported the front of the engine; behind them were four large wheels powered by piston-driven rods. This design had no unpowered wheels under the cab, hence the zero in 4–4–0. The buildings behind the engine still exist on Railroad Street. *Courtesy of Maynard Historical Society.*

Rails cross Fort Pond Brook via a wooden trestle bridge in South Acton, just south of where the spur that ran through Maynard joined to the B&M line that ran from Boston to Fitchburg.

Railroad Company had been taken over by the Boston & Maine Railroad. Passenger service to Marlborough ended in 1932, then for Hudson and Stow in 1939 and finally for Maynard in 1958. Maynard's passenger station was demolished in 1960. Freight service diminished over the years, dramatically dropping off when the American Woolen Company ceased operations in 1950.

The last freight run was sometime in the mid-1960s, although the line itself was not officially abandoned until 1979. By then, trees were growing between the rails. A few older residents of Maynard can remember walking the trestle over the river—quite a daring act, as there were no railings and the Assabet River was dozens of feet below. The railroad right-of-way from South Acton to Marlborough is the future Assabet River Rail Trail.

BACKYARD TREASURES

Old Bottles

Landscaping and remodeling around any old New England house will turn up interesting relics. Here are a few of the finds from one old house in Maynard.

One unglazed brown clay marble. For those of us who barely remember glass marbles, it is interesting to learn that until 1900 the great majority of marbles were made of not glass but clay. Akron, Ohio, was the Marble Capital of the World. The S.C. Dyke & Company and other Akron companies turned out up to a million clay marbles a day. These could be unglazed in various colors, painted, glazed and even porcelain. Unglazed marbles were referred to as common marbles to distinguish them from various fancy marbles and were often called "commies." Thus, the term predates the pejorative for members of the Communist Party.

Two glass bottles. Actually a few glass bottles, plus many fragments of glass and pottery, but two bottles have an interesting back story. The Society for Historical Archaeology (SHA) is host to the Historic Glass Bottle Identification & Information website at http://www.sha.org/bottle/index.htm. This site has a tremendous amount of information on U.S. glass bottles from early 1800s to 1950s. The first bottle is four-sided, three inches tall and

These backyard and barn finds date from the late 1800s to the early 1900s.

reads "Batchelor's No. 1 Liquid Hair Dye." The Batchelor family owned a hair dye and wig-making company in New York from the 1850s onward. Images of Civil War–era newspaper advertisements for Batchelor's hair dye can be found via Internet searches.

The second bottle is cylindrical, about four inches tall and reads "HALL'S CATARRH CURE." It has seams up both sides indicative of machine-made bottles produced after 1905. The Cheney Medicine Company bought the formula and rights to Dr. Henry Hall's Catarrh Cure in 1871 and aggressively marketed it nationally for more than thirty years. Newspapers of the era lobbied and editorialized against any regulation of the patent medicine industry because such advertising was a large part of their revenue. Catarrh, by the way, was described as inflammation of the nose and/or throat with congestion and mucus, brought on by anything from allergy, infection or the common cold.

Nails, knobs and tubes. Second-floor remodeling yielded square-cut nails and porcelain knobs and tubes. "Square" nails, as distinguished from modern-day, wire-cut, round nails, were common from 1820 to around 1910. A long, flat band of steel was fed into a stamping machine, which stamp cut each nail from the end as the band progressed into the machine. A separate machine pounded one end to make the head of the nail. It was all very noisy! "Knob-and-tube" wiring was popular from the 1890s to as late as the 1930s. Porcelain knobs were attached to joists, wall framing or rafters, and wires strung from knob to knob. For wires passing through a stud, holes were drilled and fitted with glazed or unglazed ceramic tubes to protect the wood from the heat of the conducting wires.

Chapter 6

Assabet River

Lore has it that in the low water of summer, this river was turned off on Sundays, so as to allow mill ponds to refill for powering the mills Monday through Saturday.

A River Runs Through It

Once upon a time, the Assabet River was known as the Elizabeth River, as well as Assabeth, Asabet, Elizbeth, Elizabet—all thought to be Anglicized versions of an Algonquin Indian name. The major tributary flowing from north to south through Stow is Elizabeth Brook. Before Maynard was Maynard it was Assabet Village. North of the river was part of Stow; south, part of Sudbury. Nathaniel Hawthorne, 1804–1864, lived in Concord and wrote: "Rowing our boat against the current, between wide meadows, we turn aside into the Assabeth. A more lovely stream than this, for a mile above its junction with the Concord, has never flowed on earth."

The Assabet is thirty-one miles long, from headwaters in Westborough (elevation 320 feet) to its merge with the Sudbury River to form the Concord River (elevation 100 feet). The rivers are well served by the nonprofit Organization for the Assabet, Sudbury and Concord Rivers (OARS; www.oars3rivers.org). OARS's goal is that the river be clean enough to be fishable and swimmable. Seven towns draw their well water from within the Assabet Valley watershed, and four discharge their treated wastewater into the river.

Artemas Whitney (1815–1907) built this dam for Amory Maynard and William Knight in 1847, yet it is named the Ben Smith Dam. Maybe Mr. Smith owned the land?

There are seven historic mill dams on the Assabet; Maynard's Ben Smith Dam is the largest.

The Ben Smith Dam is 9.5 feet tall and 170.0 feet wide and was built in 1847 to hold back water for Maynard's woolen mill operations. Behind it, the Assabet is backed up for five miles, almost to the Gleasondale Dam. In Maynard, Ice House Landing offers parking and a place to launch canoes or kayaks onto this quiet water. Stow has four put-in spots (see OARS's maps). The south shore is bordered by Track Road and the Assabet River National Wildlife Refuge; the north shore by Gardner Hill Forest. Both sides offer hiking opportunities. Of historical note, a steam-powered launch operated on the Assabet River from 1906 to 1914, transporting people from a dock near the Ben Smith Dam to a landing near Lake Boon.

In passing, it is worth noting that much of downtown Maynard is actually an island! The river and canal split above the Ben Smith Dam. The canal water leads to the Mill Pond, then rejoins the river east of Clock Tower Place by Walnut Street. The island is 0.7 miles long with Main Street running down the center. There are seven bridges to the island. The layout does not replicate the famed "Seven Bridges of Konigsberg" puzzle but does pose a related puzzle: is it possible to cross each bridge once and end up where you started? Ponder this puzzle while sitting on a bench in Tobin Park, behind the U.S. post office and next to the footbridge. John J. Tobin Riverfront Park is one of the few green spaces in Maynard from which to view the river.

The Assabet River as we know it may come to a radical transformation. Because of years of historical and continuing phosphorus discharge into the river, there are plant—mostly duckweed—and algae blooms during the low-water summer months. The dams act as cyclical phosphorus traps, with sedimented phosphorus taken up into plants in the summer, followed by plant death and return of phosphorus to the sediment in the winter. There is a proposal from the U.S. Army Core of Engineers to remove the dams and dredge the sediment. Of the seven historic mill dams on the Assabet, destroying the Ben Smith Dam would have the largest impact on water quality. Consequences would include the loss of the Mill Pond in Maynard and the conversion of the upstream stretch to a river twenty-five to fifty feet wide and about one foot deep. This is not in any budget yet, just a concept.

A TALE OF TWO RIVERS

"It was the best of times, it was the worst of times." So begins Dickens's *A Tale of Two Cities*. March 2010 was the best of times if you lived along the Assabet River and the worst of times near the Sudbury River. The Assabet stayed within its riverbanks, but the Sudbury flooded so widely that people were referring to it as the "Sudbury Ocean." Major commuting roads in Sudbury and Wayland were closed for days. Given that both rivers arise in Westborough, drain a similar-sized region and stretch roughly the same length before joining in Concord to form the Concord River, why were the experiences so different?

The Assabet starts in the Westborough marshes that drain into the George H. Nichols flood control basin (more on this later), then works its way first north and then east. For much of its length, the Assabet drops 5 feet for every mile. Within Maynard, river elevation is 175 feet over the top of the Ben Smith Dam and 145 feet out the east side. This drop in elevation means that water moves quickly through the Assabet watershed. Although there were four major storms in forty days, much of the high water subsided between storms. Peak heights at the official Maynard recording site were 6.4, 7.1, 5.4 and 7.1 feet for the four February and March 2010 storms. Anything over 5 feet is considered "flood."

The headwaters of the Sudbury River are less than one mile away from those of the Assabet, but this river first heads east, then north. Much of the river, especially the Wayland, Sudbury and Concord parts, drops less than 1 foot in elevation for every mile of length. From Route 20 in Sudbury to the merge with the Assabet in Concord, the elevation drop is from 118 feet to 115 feet. Flow is slow, even during a flood. As a consequence, the Sudbury barely got below flood levels between the March storms. The flood of March 31 set a new record of 13.9 feet. It was interesting to find out that on that date the wild Sudbury and well-behaved Assabet each had near-identical amounts of water flowing down river—about 2,500 cubic feet per second. Combined as the Concord River, visualize that as filling a football field to a depth of 3 feet in just over a minute, over and over again, hour after hour.

There is a history of severe floods on the Assabet River, especially before the two flood-control dams, George H. Nichols Dam and Tyler Dam,

Taken from the foot bridge over the Assabet River, facing south toward the Main Street Bridge, March 2010. This was the highest the river had been since 1987.

were completed in the 1960s. The impoundment area behind Nichols is kept partially full in order to be able to provide water to the Assabet in times of drought, but it usually has a 500,000,000-gallon flood hold-back capacity. Tyler's impoundment is kept low between floods and has a hold-back capacity of 1,800,000,000 gallons. The amounts sound huge, but the Assabet River's March peak of 2,500 cubic feet per second converts to 1,500,000,000 gallons per day! Thus, the two dams are enough to mute the worst outcomes of these ten- to twenty-year floods but not enough to prevent them completely.

Back before the flood control dams were in place, the November hurricane flood of 1927 is recorded as damaging both the dam and the bridge at what is now the Route 62 crossing. The replacement bridge dates to 1928. A flood in March of 1936 washed out the wooden bridge for Mill Street. Hurricane Diane in August 1955 brought the most rain recorded in any one month and the highest water on the Assabet since modern recordkeeping began in 1942. The river crested at 8.94 feet. No bridges were lost. More recent floods of note occurred in March 1968, cresting at 8.15 feet, and January 1979, cresting at 8.11 feet. Retirees from Digital Equipment Corporation (DEC) remember sandbagging the buildings in 1968 in an attempt to keep water out of the production facilities.

Jack MacKeen reminisced, "I have a clear mental picture of Ken Olsen, president of DEC, in suit and boots, helping place sandbags between the buildings." Afterward, DEC had the river retaining wall built higher along the lowest stretch next to the mill. The wall kept the river out of the mill in 1979.

All this detail explains why in the spring of 2010 the people living along the Assabet River were passed over, while those near the Sudbury River were smote with a record-making flood. Going forward, anyone wishing to track river activity can search on "USGS Assabet" or "USGS Sudbury." Charts show real-time height and cubic feet per second, with options to see tables of monthly averages or flood peaks over past years.

LOW WATER

A river with next to no water excites the viewer far less than high water: no sandbags, no roads impassable, no sense of invasion. Plus, understanding the cause for high water is as simple as "rain runs off," while in comparison, comprehending the causes of low water leads to overwhelmingly complicated

Same view, four months later, with 1 percent of March's peak flow.

nuances about groundwater, wastewater, evaporation, evapotranspiration, aquifers and so on. And yet, there are things to know whenever the Assabet River slows to a trickle.

First the facts: the peak of the two March 2010 floods saw 2,500 cubic feet per second rushing through downtown Maynard. That's 18,700 gallons a second, 1.1 million per minute, 67.3 million per hour or 1,616 million gallons of water per day. For comparison, Maynard's water usage is just under 1.0 million gallons per day. The July 2010 drought found the river as low as 17 cubic feet per second, i.e., less than 1 percent of that peak flow. The U.S. Geological Survey records show a March average of 401 cubic feet per second based on sixty-eight years of record-keeping and a July average of 76 cubic feet per second. Record lows for summer droughts are under 5 cubic feet per second.

Low water on the Assabet River is not due to less rain during the summer months. The watershed averages close to four inches of precipitation every month (see figure). Yet the spring peak flow averages more than four times the summer low. Even allowing for the spring snowmelt contribution to that spring peak, summer flow is lower than might be expected. But more of summer rain evaporates or only replenishes local groundwater without reaching the river aquifer. Plants take up water and, via evapotranspiration, release that moisture into the air. A single large tree can release several hundred gallons of water per day; an acre of grass, far more. An eighteen-hole golf course might irrigate 500,000 gallons per day, with much of that lost from the local watershed to evaporation and evapotranspiration.

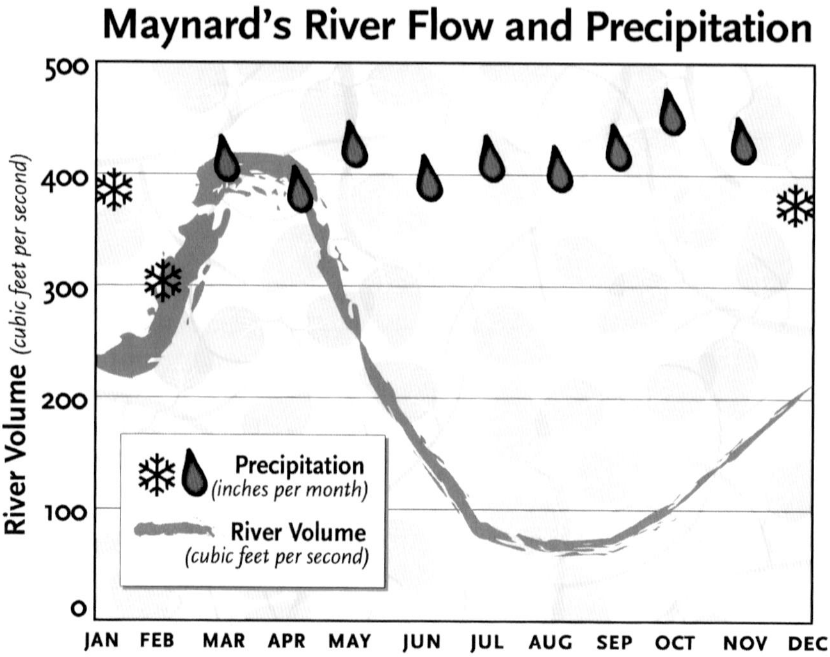

Average precipitation is four inches a month, but average river flow is more than four times higher in March and April than in the summer months. *Created by Felice Katz.*

Low water reveals trash. Downstream of the Elks building there are still scores of old car tires visible in the river despite the Organization for the Assabet, Sudbury and Concord Rivers having conducted annual cleanups, removing hundreds of tires from just that section. Tobin Park shoreline is littered with broken glass. Clean up glass; rake a bit, more glass. Rake more, more glass. It's glass all the way down. Recent postflood finds there included an intact 6.5-ounce Coca-Cola bottle, with "LOWELL L MASS" on the bottom, date unknown.

Low water reveals fish. Maynard's section of the Assabet is home to white suckers, golden shiners and various types of sunfish. The period of late morning to early afternoon is a good time for fish sightings from the Main Street Bridge or the footbridge. Spotting fish from above can be difficult. One trick is to scan the bottom for a moving shadow, then look above the shadow for the fish. Great Blue Herons stalk these shallows for fish, crayfish and the occasional duckling.

Back in the day when mills operated on water power, some rivers were shut off nights and Sundays. These no-flow times allowed mill ponds to refill with water to power the next work shift. With multiple mills operated on the Assabet and its tributaries, there had to be cooperation among the mill operators so that everyone had water when they needed it.

A not-so-secret secret about the Assabet River is that by midsummer's low water, much of the water flowing through Maynard is cleaned water that was discharged by three upstream wastewater treatment plants. Maynard's cleaned discharge is added to the river just before it enters Acton.

Historic Floods

Imagine yourself standing facing upstream on the middle of the bridge on Maynard's Main Street. The Assabet River at this point is barely fifty feet wide. The watershed draining into this narrow gap is 114 square miles in area. The historic floods described below were usually the result of a one-two punch: one storm system or winter thaw to saturate the ground, followed closely by a second storm dumping huge amounts of rain. A not-impossible storm of four inches of rain on saturated or bare and frozen ground would mean eight billion gallons of water headed your way. Maybe standing in the middle of the bridge is not such a good idea after all!

It helps to think of the Assabet as a short, steep river. The length from headwaters in Westborough to the convergence with the Sudbury River,

Ben Smith Dam in March 2010, when 2,500 cubic feet per second of water was flowing over the top of the dam. Because water is always flowing over the top of this dam, it does not contribute to flood control capacity.

in Concord, is just over thirty miles. The elevation at headwaters is 320 feet, dropping to 100 feet at the convergence. Averaging 7 feet of descent per mile puts the Assabet in stark contrast to the Sudbury River, which for long stretches through Wayland, Sudbury and Concord drops less than 1 foot per mile. Historically, steep rivers got mill towns while flat rivers got farming villages. A combination of looking at U.S. Geological Survey data and traditional historical sources leads to an understanding of why and how the Assabet still floods every fifteen years or so, despite flood control dams.

Using Geological Survey data: Internet searching on "Assabet USGS" will find access to U.S. Geological Survey data on the Assabet River from 1941 to the present. The default display shows real-time graphs of flow in cubic feet per second plus height in feet for the most recent 7-day period, but there is an option to extend the graphed interval up to 120 days. The cubic feet per second graph also has symbols showing median flow. A table underneath provides lowest and highest on record for that date, twentieth and eightieth percentiles, median and mean.

Other data options are accessed through "summary of all available data for this site." The Annual Statistics selection shows an average flow for the past seventy years at slightly more than two hundred cubic feet per second; in drought years, half that. During the depths of summer droughts, the flow can fall below five cubic feet per second. As one cubic foot equals 7.5 gallons, the two hundred cubic feet per second average equates to 130 million gallons per day. The 2010 flood peaked at 1.6 trillion gallons per day. Assabet watershed water consumption is estimated at 10 million gallons per day, so the peak day was equivalent to more than five months of normal water usage.

Peak Streamflow, viewed as a table, identifies the past floods as occurring on August 20, 1955; March 19, 1968; January 26, 1979; April 7, 1987; and March 15, 2010. Those peak water heights were 8.94, 8.15, 8.11, 7.14 and 7.11 feet, respectively. Daily Statistics further details flow on the days leading up to and after each flood peak. Worth noting is how often the flood was preceded by water levels that were already above the annual average of two hundred cubic feet per second, signifying saturated soil, and also how quickly water rose to flood levels. In each instance, the water level rose to peak flood in less than forty-eight hours.

All of this flow information comes from a gauge situated next to the river in downtown Maynard, to the back and right of the Tedeschi Food Mart parking lot. The gauge, formally named Hydrologic Unit 01070005, is 142 feet above sea level. Drainage area upstream of this gage is 114 square miles. The drained area is not the same as the complete drainage basin of 177 square miles for the entire Assabet because significant downstream tributaries—the Fort Pond, Nashoba and Spencer Brooks—merge with the Assabet River before it in turn merges with the Sudbury River.

Using historic newspaper accounts: Maynard's public library has microfilm copies of most past issues of local newspapers. Articles pertaining to floods were found for 1927 and 1968.

- **1927**: According to the National Weather Service,

> *The 1927 hurricane season brought a tropical storm that swept northward across western New England on Nov. 3–4, 1927. As its warm, humid air rose over the mountains and hills, torrential rains fell, causing severe flooding over extensive areas in virtually all of northern New England and the upper Hudson basin in New York. Much of New England had been soaked by rains throughout October. In all, 85 people were lost.*

Photo of the damaged Waltham Street Bridge in 1927, taken from the vantage point of where the McDonald's restaurant is now situated. *Courtesy of Maynard Historical Society.*

Locally, the November 11, 1927 issue of the *Maynard News* reported bridges damaged and water flooding the mill buildings closest to the river and also the gunpowder factory a bit farther east on Powdermill Road. The Waltham Street Bridge, situated next to what is now Tedeschi Food Mart, had been built in 1840 and then widened to add an electric trolley track and sidewalk circa 1900. It was severely damaged by the flood. The replacement bridge was dated 1928; replacement of that bridge began in 2011.

Upriver, the November 4 issue of the same newspaper reported that Hudson sustained considerable flooding. Water from the Assabet backed up into the historic tannery canal. Water from Danforth Brook raised the level of Bruces Pond, which drains over the dam behind Larkin Lumber into the same canal. The combination of rising river and brook put Hudson's Main Street under three feet of water. Most of the factories and dwellings near the Assabet River were flooded. The March 2010 flood overflowed the canal again but not as severely. When questioned in October, local teens remembered that water had flowed onto the skateboard park, next to the canal.

- **1936:** "The Great Flood" was described as the worst flood in New England since 1850. Damage in Massachusetts—mostly in central and western areas—was estimated at in excess of $200 million. In today's dollars, that would have been billions. The winter of 1935–1936 had been hard, with deep snowfall and long cold snaps that turned streams and rivers to solid ice. Spring came early, with mild weather and heavy rain. By mid-March, rivers were rising across the state. On the Connecticut River, the eight-hundred-foot-long wooden covered bridge at Montague, Massachusetts, built in 1870, was lifted off its pilings by the high water and moved downriver in one piece, taking out railroad bridges as it went. Locally, bridges were damaged and roads washed out. Two years later, the famous "Long Island Express" hurricane of 1938 resulted in local wind damage, but the heaviest rains were in western Massachusetts.

- **1955**: Hurricane Diane dropped more than 12.0 inches of rain on eastern Massachusetts in just three days. Jean Duggan, lifelong Maynard resident, remembers that "in August of 1955 my parents brought me to see water flowing over the Waltham Street bridge. We stood on the south side." The high water crest of 8.94 feet from Hurricane Diane was the highest the river has been since recordkeeping began in 1942. Perhaps Mrs. Duggan's parents were remembering the 1927 flood in their own childhood, when that Waltham Street bridge was damaged. August 1955 remains the rainiest month on record, although the multiple storms of March 2010 got close.
- **1968 and 1979**: These were the first serious floods after flood control dams were built on the upper Assabet River and its tributaries. Both exceeded 8.1 feet. The first put water over the retaining wall next to Maynard's Mill, necessitating frantic sandbagging and pumping to save Digital Equipment Corporation. The March 21, 1968 issue of the *Assabet Valley Beacon* has a lengthy report on damage in Maynard and surrounding towns, plus many pictures. Afterward, DEC had the river retaining wall on its side of the river built higher. The wall kept the river out of the mill during the equally high flood of January 1979, but Walnut Street was again under water, and the AT&T building on the east side of Walnut Street was sandbagged to keep water out. A lesser flood in April 1987 was barely higher than the 7.1 feet experienced in March 2010.

Impact of the historic mill dams: In Maynard, seven bridges cross the Assabet below the Ben Smith Dam, built circa 1850. The view from all of them finds river flow through Maynard is clear water over a primarily stony bottom draped in algae and waterweeds, the reason being that most of the upstream sediment is trapped above the dam. Sediment thickness toward the west end of the Ben Smith dam impoundment, by Crow Island, is four to eight feet thick. Nearer the Ben Smith Dam, sediment is one to four feet thick.

The impoundment area upstream of the Ben Smith Dam, the Mill Pond and the large parking lots surrounding Clock Tower Place and downtown Maynard contribute to flash flood potential through and below Maynard because any rain on those sites gets into the river very quickly. Boon Lake's overflow also adds to fast-rising water downstream. The Assabet gauge typically shows a sharp upward spike after every heavy rainfall, followed by a sharp downward drop soon after the rain stops, followed later by a slow rise as water from the upstream tributaries enters the river.

The other historic mill dams on the Assabet, in varying states of disrepair, are the Aluminum City Dam at Route 20 in Northborough, Allen Street Dam, Hudson Dam just upstream of Route 85, Gleasondale Dam near Route 62 and, then downstream of Maynard, the Powdermill Dam and the remnants of the breached Damonmill Dam. "Aluminum City" is its name because it is next to a store that sells aluminum doors and windows. All of these dams have continuous flow and do not significantly restrain floodwater for later dispersal. Likewise, historic mill dams on the tributaries, such as the dam at Larkin Lumber, mentioned earlier, are continuous flow—i.e., over-the-top dams—and do not contribute to flood control. Armeno Coffee Roasters on Otis Road, Northborough, occupies the mill building that was once powered by the water of Hop Brook, held back by a small dam to create Smith Pond, which is also continuous flow.

Flood control dams of Nichols, Tyler and others: Flood control projects are designed to hold back water in times of heavy rain. A series of Atlantic hurricanes in the 1950s led to construction of local flood control dams in the 1960s and 1970s. The George H. Nichols Dam, Westborough, was completed in 1968. Its reservoir of a bit more than half a square mile serves as a recreational boating and fishing site. It also serves as a supply of water for the Assabet River in times of drought. This earthen dam is next to the Westboro Country Club, just north of Route 30. In times of high water, what backs up behind the dam is released slowly through the spillway outlet. Funding from the Federal Recovery Act was used over 2010–2011 to bring the dam up to current safety and performance standards, thus reducing the risk of future flood damage downstream.

Tyler Dam is on Robin Hill Street in Marlborough, about a mile south of the Solomon Pond Mall. It was constructed in 1965. Tyler Dam is designed to not obstruct any flow during normal river conditions and only backs up water into the otherwise swampy impoundment area in times of flood risk. The flood hold-back capacities of these two dams are 500 million and 1.8 trillion gallons, respectively. The amounts sound huge, but the Assabet River's March 2010 peak of 2,500 cubic feet per second at Maynard's gauge converts to 1.62 trillion gallons per day. And that gauge is upstream of fully one-third of the river's entire drainage basin.

In addition to these two major flood control installations on the Assabet River proper, there are other flood control contributions on some of the tributaries. The Delaney Complex, on the Stow-Harvard border, was completed in 1971. It consists of a six-hundred-foot-long earthen dike with an outlet channel. Others are created not by dams but by deliberately narrow channels backing up into undeveloped swampy areas. The channels were constructed where brooks cross under roads. Both Cold Harbor Brook and Hop Brook, in Northborough, have areas on the map designated as "Fc" for flood control, as does Barefoot Brook, near Solomon Pond Mall. In Berlin, the Ross Site Fc and Brewer Brook Area are flood-control projects on North Brook. Lake Boon, in Stow, will rise one foot before overflowing the earthen dike that serves as its dam. The narrow bridge over Fort Pond Brook at Route 27, Acton, serves as flood control, as do the spillways on Nashoba Brook in West Concord, backing up water in Warner's Pond. Collectively, these tributary flood control projects hold back more than the 2.3 trillion gallons of the two "major" flood control installations.

In retrospect, the March 2010 flood was not a one-hundred-year flood, a fifty-year flood or even a twenty-five-year flood. Records show that about every ten to twenty years or so, either a fall hurricane or spring rains conspire to drop billions of gallons of water on our part of Massachusetts. Flood-control efforts take the edge off flood peaks but cannot prevent them entirely.

Chapter 7

Mammals

People in eastern Massachusetts no longer hunt, trap, skin or eat wild mammals—well, most of them don't. Their dogs are on leashes and their cats are too well fed to do more than recreational stalking. As a result, small- to large-sized mammals have moved back into the neighborhood. Expect skunks, raccoons and opossums; don't be surprised to see coyotes and deer.

Life under the Snow

Snow—serious snow covering the earth six inches or more and lingering for months—is a boon to some of the small life that stays active all winter because snow insulates. In between soil and snow, the temperatures hover around 32 degrees even when surface temperatures are in single digits or colder. Snow also shields from sight. Voles and shrews start making paths under the covering snow to search for food. The snow protects them from hawks and other surface hunters such as cats. These tunnels are invisible from the surface as long as the snow remains deep, but when snow thins during a thaw, the tunnels become visible as dark, meandering lines an inch or two across. Look for them on lawns, mowed fields and in the rough on golf courses.

Voles, often referred to as field or meadow mice, are plant eaters. Their diet is mostly roots and seeds. Under deep snow cover they will gnaw at the bark of shrubs and young trees, girdling and thus killing the plants. Orchard owners put protective mesh collars around young trees. Populations are

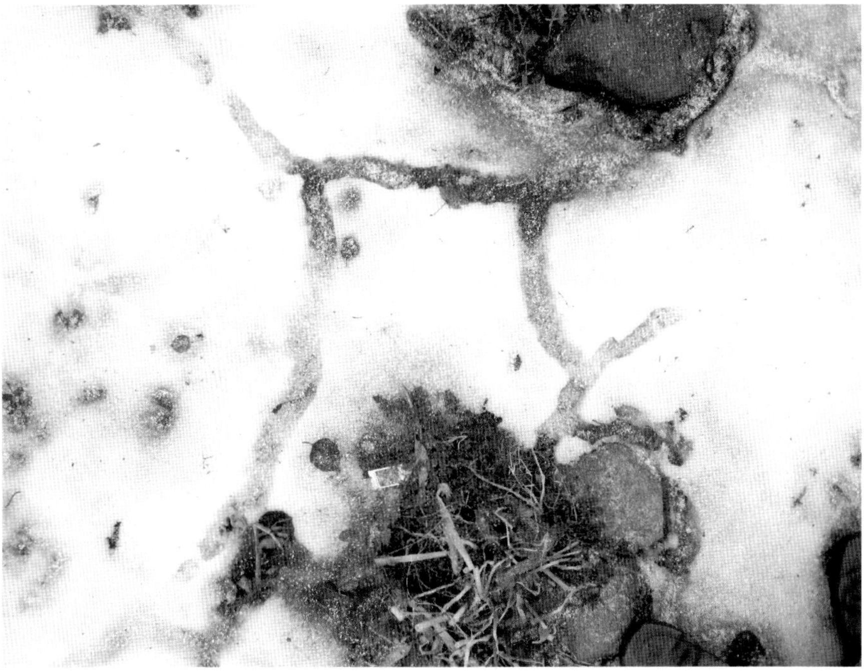

At the end of the snow season, melting reveals mouse tunnels.

usually a few dozen per acre, but there can be periodic population booms when counts exceed two hundred per acre. Naturally, predator booms follow. In the far north, there appears to be a four-year boom/bust cycle of lemmings, voles and owls. When the rodent population crashes, the owls will fly far outside their normal range in search of food, referred to as an irruption. The Mass Audubon Society notes that snowy owls show up as far south as Massachusetts.

Shrews are hyperactive carnivores. The northern short-tailed shrew eats half or more of its body weight each day. Shrews prefer earthworms, but as worms migrate downward to avoid winter freezing temperatures, the winter-active shrews not only go after snails, slugs, insects, grubs and small vertebrates such as salamanders and frogs but also mice and voles. The saliva of short-tailed shrews is poisonous. It contains a neurotoxin that subdues prey similar in size to the shrew or even larger, such as adult voles. Life in those snow tunnels can be a dire state of hunter versus the hunted.

Death also comes from above. Although the subnivean lifestyle provides visual cover, it is not absolute protection against all hunters. Great gray owls, flying low over the snow, can hear scurrying noises in the tunnels and then crash the roof with their talons. Similarly, fox and coyotes pounce down on the sound with paws or jaws and come up with a mouthful of snow and vole.

Wood frogs and spring peeper frogs are also under the snow but with a different survival strategy. As winter approaches, these frogs sequester large amounts of glucose and urea in their cells. This change to their biochemistry has a dual purpose: as an antifreeze and to reduce damage to cells as water between the cells crystallizes into ice. The end result is that frogs tucked into the decaying leaves on the forest floor either don't freeze at all if the snow cover is good or freeze in a nondamaging and reversible manner. The over-wintering female frog is already full of eggs. Once spring temperatures rise about forty degrees, the same frogs that in winter's cold have neither heartbeat nor breath will in effect turn "on" again and move toward the vernal pond in which they were born to meet, mate and leave fertilized eggs.

So for many New England species, the response to "Did you have a good winter?" is "Did it snow enough?" And when it begins to warm, that female frog—that sleeping beauty—will welcome the kiss of spring. The alternative, being found too soon by a voracious shrew, would be another type of kiss entirely.

COYOTES

The Wolves Are Back in Town

One hundred years ago, Massachusetts had no wolves—they had been hunted to local extinction. Coyotes were not here yet. Their territory was mostly west of the Mississippi River. During the middle of the last century, coyotes started appearing in upstate New York and, as time went on, spread to the New England states. Today, most town woods, large parks and golf courses have coyotes in residence. Sightings are common within Boston city limits. Estimates are that there are five thousand to ten thousand coyotes in Massachusetts. But are these western coyotes migrating east, or are they something else entirely?

The answer: something else. Anyone who has visited Arizona or New Mexico knows the coyote as a twenty-five- to thirty-five-pound, midtier predator more comfortable in open country than woodlands. What we have locally and in neighboring towns are larger coyotes, more on the order of thirty to fifty pounds. Their coats are thicker, their jaws are wider and stronger and they look a bit like slimmed-down, long-legged German shepherds. In the vacuum left by the absence of wolves, they are the apex predator. Although much of what they eat is still small game, they are successful hunters of deer.

As it turns out, our local coyotes are coyote-wolf hybrids (coywolves). DNA analysis confirms that coyotes migrated from the plains states northward into Ontario and Quebec about eighty to one hundred years ago, where they mated with remnant populations of red wolves. Small numbers of these coyote-wolves crossed the St. Lawrence Seaway to New York, either during winter ice over or perhaps on bridges. This fast-growing, east-spreading population has been referred to as a "hybrid swarm." Purebred "western" coyotes also moved east across Ohio and western Pennsylvania but more slowly and without the size change. Earlier arguments that what we see in the east are coyote-dog hybrids do not stand up to examination. The genes don't match. Furthermore, both coyotes and red wolves mate in late winter for spring litters, plus males actively partake in feeding and caring of pups—two traits not seen in dogs. In Pennsylvania, the purebred and hybrid populations are converging from opposite ends of the state. The question going forward is which one will win out, genetically.

What does it mean that wolves, in the form of these coyote-wolves, are back in New England? Hunting pressure by coyote-wolves is beginning to slow the runaway deer population, as well as the runaway Canada geese population, although purebred coyotes manage that just as well in the Midwest. Pressure is also increased on the feral cat population and probably wild turkey, rabbits, opossums, woodchucks and more. In suburban and urban areas, the culprit tipping over garbage cans is more likely to be coyotes than a bear or raccoons. A small plus is that they clean up roadkill.

Being a good neighbor to your local coywolf means not putting food outside for your pets. Letting a cat out for the night is bad odds for getting that cat back in the morning. Walk your dog on a leash, especially in the woods. At home, a five-foot-tall fenced-in yard should be enough to protect your pets, chickens and other animals. Coyotes and coyote-wolves are less averse to living near human habitat than pure wolves, but they still tend to be shy. A coyote hanging out in broad daylight may be injured, ill or have rabies and should be reported to the police, who will forward the information to the animal control officer.

Jonathan G. Way has spent years studying coyotes in eastern Massachusetts and elsewhere. His book, *Suburban Howls*, is a great read. He is trying to establish a no-hunting, coywolf wildlife refuge on Cape Cod. He also operates www.easterncoyoteresearch.com, a very informative website.

SKUNKS

Maynard is home to an estimated 75 to 150 skunks. Skunks have adapted admirably to suburban/rural habitat, especially when old farm fields, forest and access to open water are part of the habitat.

Every March the male striped skunks come out of their winter torpor to start wandering in search of females. Females winter together in groups of three to eight. This communal huddling shares body warmth and helps preserve body fat needed for a spring pregnancy. Females relocate to solo dens to raise their families. The kits, typically four to eight per litter, are born in early June. By mid-July the kits are large enough to leave the den to feed, trooping after their mother. Dad skunk has no role in raising the kits. Lifespan in the wild is on the order of two to five years. For skunks kept as pets (not legal in Massachusetts), lifespan is more like eight to twelve years.

Skunks are crepuscular, which is not the same as nocturnal. The former refers to foraging for food during the twilight hours after sunset and before dawn but not during the darkest hours of night. Skunks roam distances of a mile or more each night. They tend to return to the same den before sunrise. Skunks will eat just about anything: insects, grubs, fruit, berries, eggs, mice and more. If kitchen scraps go to a compost bin that is animal accessible, there will be skunks.

The name "skunk" derives from the Algonquin Indian name, variously transliterated as "seganku," "segongw" or "sekakwa." Translations range from "one who squirts" to "squirting fox" or "urinating fox." What skunks squirt is a mixture of sulfur-containing compounds known as thiols or mercaptans. The smell is so repulsive that few scientists have been willing to conduct research on this subject, and even if they are willing, their peers, students and families complain.

The Ho-Chunk Indians have a skunk origin story. A girl was born with all-white hair. She grew to be beautiful but vain. She would rub herself with flowers to capture their scent and gaze at herself in still water's reflection. One day a stranger arrived—an ugly man. She rejected him. But he was the great spirit Turtle in disguise. He addressed her: "Since you rejected one of the great spirits, you shall be transformed into a lowly animal! When people see you, they will turn away from your repulsive odor." She shrank to animal size, and her skin became covered with black hair. The only trace left of her beautiful white hair was the white stripe down her back.

In Massachusetts, skunks are second only to raccoons for confirmed cases of rabid animals. Raccoon rabies tends to spike every five to eight years;

the last spike was 2004–2005. Raccoon rabies spills over into the skunk population because the habitat and habits of the two species overlap. Given that skunks strongly avoid daylight, the first sign that a skunk has rabies is walking around during the day. Other common signs are lack of fear or actual aggressiveness toward humans, dogs or other animals. In 2010, the Massachusetts Department of Public Health documented 131 rabid animals, out of 2,418 tested. The top three were raccoons at 61, skunks at 28 and bats at 14. No dogs tested positive in 2010, which is a testament to the value of rabies vaccination.

Odds and ends: "Skunked," as in "We were skunked," refers to being defeated in a sports contest without scoring at all. Skunked beer happens when hops compounds in beer are exposed to ultraviolet light (as in sunlight), and the decomposition releases sulfur compounds that smell, well, skunky. If you are of a certain age, you can remember Loudon Wainwright III singing "Dead Skunk in the Middle of the Road" on the radio. The song's popularity peaked in the spring of 1973, as the Watergate investigation of President Nixon's involvement continued to heat up. Loudon refused to say whether there was a connection.

Deer

Six years ago, a *New York Times* Science section article claimed that bee/wasp/hornet stings caused forty to eighty human deaths per year—more deaths than all other animal species combined. The *New York Times* was wrong. As pointed out in a letter to the editor, deer were responsible for approximately 150 deaths per year. That number has risen. Government and the insurance industry reports now put the number of deaths at more than 200 per year, plus 20,000 injuries, plus more than a billion dollars of vehicular damage. How can a species that was hunted to scarcity one hundred years ago be causing so much havoc?

Estimates for the precolonial deer population are that ten to twenty million white-tailed deer roamed North America. Does give birth to one to two fawns in the spring. Fawns that survive the first winter will be sexually mature the next fall, although the young males are usually excluded from mating by dominant older males. Normal lifespan in the wild is five to nine years. Adult weights range from 70 to 150 pounds for females and 100 to 250 pounds for males. Those weights don't sound large enough to lead to the death of a person in the car, but the statistics include accidents caused by people swerving to avoid a deer and those who hit a deer and then lost control of the car or motorcycle.

Historically, deer predators were wolves, mountain lions and humans. Native Americans used deer for food, clothing and tools. Meat not eaten fresh was dried for jerky or mixed with rendered fat to make pemmican. The arriviste European colonists also viewed deer as food but additionally as crop-raiding pests able to jump fences built to keep cattle, horses and pigs out of the fields of wheat, corn and other crops.

Hundreds of years of clearing land for farming plus unlicensed hunting put severe pressure on the deer population; by 1900, estimates were that fewer than 500,000 white-tailed deer were alive in the United States. The Massachusetts population could have been less than 1,000. Over subsequent years, states banned commercial hunting and sale of venison and also established regulations for licensed sports hunting. Deer were reintroduced to areas where they had been eliminated. With a dearth of natural predators plus the abandonment and rewilding of farmland, the deer population in the United States is now estimated at 25 to 30 million.

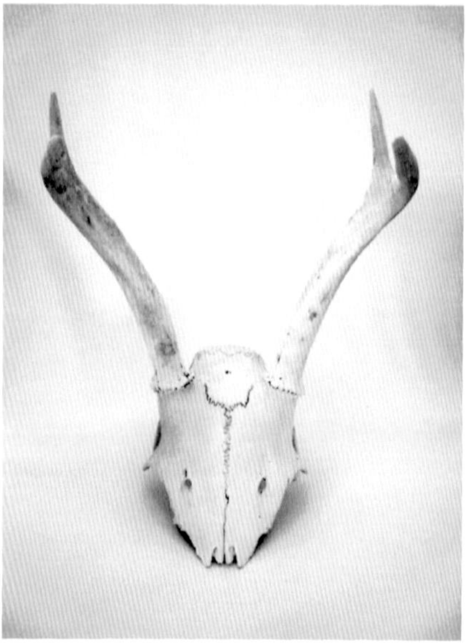

This partial skull was found underwater near the edge of a lake. Given that the antlers were still attached, this male probably fell through the ice and drowned in the late fall before the ice was thick enough to be safe, rather than during the spring thaw, as antlers would have already been shed by spring.

Current goals for Massachusetts are to maintain the wild deer population at 80,000 to 100,000. This works out to a bit over 10 deer per square mile of land surface area. Densities in semirural eastern Massachusetts towns can be more on the order of 15 to 30 per square mile. This math leads to estimates of 600 deer in Stow and 100 in Maynard. Problem areas in New Jersey, Pennsylvania and other states can exceed 50 per square mile. Since 1990, Massachusetts has been licensing 8,000 to 12,000 deer to be killed by hunters each year as a means of population management. Deer hunting, in which the season runs from mid-October to the end of December (never on Sundays), is limited to bows, shotguns and muzzle-loading rifles. In Pennsylvania, the first day of hunting season is an unofficial school holiday in many towns, and the annual harvest exceeds 500,000.

Winter walks are good for spotting deer tracks in snow or frozen mud. If you are lucky enough to come across a rotting deer carcass, return with a heavy-duty plastic bag and rubber gardening gloves. Collect the interesting bones: head, spine, ribs, scapula and pelvis. Once home, fill a five gallon bucket with water, add as many bones as will fit, cover securely with the bucket lid, drill a few holes to vent and let it sit out in the sun. After a week, dump the water, hose off the loose stuff and repeat the soak. Once the bones are almost entirely free of soft tissue, immerse them overnight in 3 percent hydrogen peroxide. Quarts can be purchased at any pharmacy. Scrape off remaining soft tissue with a knife, repeat the soak with fresh hydrogen peroxide and let dry. If you're not a do-it-yourselfer, contact Bad to the Bone Skull Cleaning. They do deer skulls for about $100.

Tracks in the Snow

Mornings after a light snow are good times to learn what animals are frequenting your yard or perhaps your favorite walk in the woods. Raccoons are active in the dim-lit hours after dusk and before sunrise, as are mice, rabbits, skunks and deer. Predators such as cats and coyotes need to be out when their prey are out, so ditto. All of these species create tracks from where they find safe shelter to their food sources and to open water. MassWildlife has a great animal tracks guide available online at http://www.mass.gov/dfwele/dfw/wildlife/publications/tracks_guide.pdf.

White-tailed deer: There's no mistaking this footprint. Females are high steppers, while males tend to be foot draggers. Until late January, a live sighting will confirm the difference, as males are still sporting their antlers even though breeding season ended in early December. Fawns arrive in June. By then, males will have already begun to grow their antlers for the coming fall.

Cats: Claws retracted; foot and four toes. Also, cats have that runway model habit of swinging each foot into the centerline before putting it down, so the footprints line up almost single file.

Skunks: Compared to a cat's footprints, a skunk's is five-toed, claw marks showing and hind foot larger than front foot. The walk is more of a waddle. Look for trails next to fences, hedges, buildings and stone walls.

Mice, moles, shrews and voles: Think small. Once snow cover is deep enough, these smaller mammals will establish trails that are actually under the snow, next to the ground's surface. While visually hidden, the acute hearing of foxes and coyotes allow these predators to crash through the snow to their intended prey. Deer mice and white-footed mice are larger than house mice; their trails in light snow are distinguished by tail-dragging marks between the footprints.

Squirrels: Easy to spot near bird feeders, these marks are distinctive because when at their leisure, squirrels prefer to hop rather than step. Squirrels can switch to a high-speed scramble when being pursued by a cat or dog.

Coyotes and dogs: One will be accompanied by human footprints; the other, not. Even off the leash on a walk in the woods, a dog's trail will wander way from the human trail but always return; however, if you are the first human into the woods on a snowy morning and there are already a dog's footprints down the trail ahead of you, it wasn't a dog. Look for footprints of a size and spacing you would expect from a small, anorexic-looking German shepherd. Mark Twain made an apt observation in *Roughing It*: "The cayote [*sic*] is a living, breathing allegory of Want. He is always hungry. He is always poor, out of luck and friendless. The meanest creatures despise him."

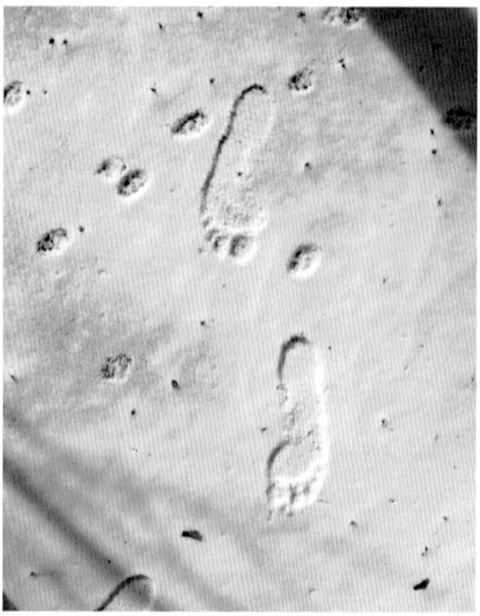

Night snow, viewed in the early morning, shows evidence of both night and early morning walkers. In this case, a cat's path was later crossed by a human out to pick up the morning newspaper.

Humans: Hopefully not in your yard, but farther afield, look for boot marks, ski tracks and snowshoe stompings. The last two may be flanked on both sides by circular holes punched in the snow every two to four feet from ski poles. Rarer, also look for signs of a bicycle, either from a standard mountain bike tread or from a spiked tire designed especially for snow and ice. Humans have also been known to roll snow into balls. Look for a large area of disturbed snow near balls of snow as much as two or three feet in diameter. These may be stacked on top of each other and decorated with sticks. Function unknown.

Chapter 8

TWENTIETH CENTURY

Prior to federal Prohibition, Maynard was still "wet" when the surrounding towns had voted themselves "dry." This meant lots of business for the intertown trolley. Much later, cars were the means to get to Erikson's for ice cream on a hot summer night.

THE *MAYNARD NEWS*

1911

One hundred years ago, the weekly local newspaper was the *Maynard News*, servicing the towns of Maynard, Hudson, South Acton, Stow and Concord Junction (West Concord). The Maynard Public Library has many of the 1911 issues available on microfilm. What is surprising is how little actual "news" was in the paper. Week after week, the front page was filled with announcement-type items, such as a wrestling match at the Finnish Hall, a lecture on the "White Slave Trade," engagement announcements and school concerts.

Here are a few summarized selections from the rarer newsworthy items:

March 10: The body of John Scott of Stow was discovered in the woods near the Assabet River on March 5. Scott had been working at the ice harvest for the JR Bent icehouse, near what is now Ice House Landing, Maynard. He was sent home early on January 24 because his clothes had gotten all wet.

Maynard Drama Society, 1910. They may be "in costume," as at least two of the men appear to be wearing wigs. Theater productions would have been advertised in the newspaper. *Courtesy of Maynard Historical Society.*

He never arrived. Scott, fifty-two years old and unmarried, had the habit of being away from home for long periods of time, so his brother had not reported him missing. It appeared that he had slipped while crossing over a stone wall, was knocked unconscious and then froze to death.

March 17: Maynard voted to stay "wet" on the issue of local option Prohibition, with the vote tally at 467 to 340. A week earlier, Hudson, which had been dry, voted itself wet again. Prohibiting alcohol was a bottom-up strategy—not "bottoms up." Starting shortly before 1900, the Anti-Saloon League developed a strategy of campaigning for individual towns and counties to vote themselves "dry," meaning the manufacture or sale of alcohol would be locally prohibited. All this led to Prohibition going into effect nationwide in 1920. Prohibition proved to be wildly unpopular and was repealed in 1933. Localities could still vote themselves dry. Lincoln, Weston and Harvard were still dry as of 2007 but are now all wet.

March 31: Phineas Feather, former superintendent of the Gleasondale Mills, in Stow, attempted to murder Alfred Gleason, mill owner. At the mill headquarters, he confronted Gleason over money he felt due him and then drew a revolver from his pocket. Mill superintendent Charles E. Roberts was shot through the chest, and although severely wounded, he disarmed Feather and, with Gleason's help, wrestled him to the floor. Robert J. Bevis

Maynard's firemen, posing on an unpaved Main Street with the hose wagon—the other major piece of equipment was a ladder wagon. Horse power served until 1914. The ability to grow a mustache appeared to be a job requirement. *Courtesy of Maynard Historical Society.*

and others ran into the office to help subdue Feather. During the struggle, Bevis and Feather were both shot, in the hand and arm, respectively, by a second gun Feather drew from another pocket. Feather was arrested. Roberts survived his injury.

April 21: A derailment of a Boston & Maine passenger train occurred in Maynard on Sunday afternoon, April 16, 1911. The train was approaching Maynard from the west, had just crossed Great Road (Route 117) and was parallel to High Street when the tender and the two passenger cars went off the rails. The passenger cars tipped onto their sides. Several passengers were injured. Mr. Larkin, who was traveling with his wife and children, told the newspaper reporter that he was "thoroughly incensed" at the engineer for driving unnecessarily fast. Souvenir hunters came directly from church services to take parts from the wrecked cars as mementos. Professional photographers arrived to take photos for the Boston newspapers and to sell as picture postcards. The Maynard Historical Society has pictures of the wreck posted in its on-line archive.

Advertisements: Distasio's Market offered beef at $0.15 to $0.25 per pound. Lerer's Clothing Store had men's shoes for $2.00 and suits for $10.00 to $20.00. Another ad offered an oak dining room table with six chairs for only $25.00. The 1911 models of the Mitchell Car, which were offered by the Mitchell-Lewis Car Company of Racine, Wisconsin, were priced from $1,200.00 to $2,250.00 and delivered thirty to fifty horsepower. In the fall, Ford Motor Company offered the 1912 models starting at $690.00. To put all this into perspective, factory pay was less than $2.00 a day.

MAYNARD'S ELECTRIC TROLLEY

1901 to 1923

A resident with ninety-five years or more behind them, plus a sharp memory, might just remember when an electric trolley ran through Maynard and Stow. Electric trolleys represented cutting-edge technology of that era. In 1890, the city of Boston had a horse-drawn trolley system, known then as the West End Street Railway Company. West End had two thousand cars in service and employed as many as nine thousand horses. At the same time, West End was actively researching the recently developed electric power technology that would allow centralized power plants to power electric motors on each trolley car. West End's Central Power Station, at the time

Initially, half the cars on the Concord, Maynard & Hudson Street Railway were open sided, and half were closed. Open-sided cars had benches all the way across. Conductors walked on the outside step to collect fares. In one of two recorded fatal accidents, Conductor Walter White lost his grip while the trolley was crossing the Concord River, went over the bridge railing, and drowned. *Collection of Robert C. Swaney.*

the largest electric station in the world, went online in 1891. Transition was so fast that the last horse was retired in 1897.

Locally, the Concord, Maynard & Hudson Street Railway (CM&H) incorporated in 1899, started construction in the spring of 1901 and had initial test runs in August 1901. In the first month of operation, CM&H was running 20 cars on 8.6 miles of track, and carried 52,347 passengers. By 1911 CM&H had merged with the Concord & Clinton and the Lowell, Acton & Maynard Street Railways and was operating trolleys from Concord to Hudson via Maynard and Stow, with a spur through South Acton all the way to West Acton. It took about an hour to get from Concord to Hudson for a total of twenty cents. At the Concord end, passengers could transfer to trains to Boston; at the Hudson end, where the rotary is now, passengers could transfer to trolleys to Marlborough or Worcester. All of this was later merged into Massachusetts Consolidated Railways.

CM&H operated custom-built luxury cars for rent, in addition to the standard open-sided or closed passenger cars. Think of those luxury cars as the party limousines of the day. Each of the three cars—the Concord,

Maynard and Hudson—had carpeting, wicker chairs, electric lights and curtained windows. These private cars could be hired for trips and were not limited to CM&H rails. There is a record of a day trip to Woonsocket, Rhode Island!

Individual towns and states were voting themselves "dry" prior to the 1919 passage of national Prohibition against the sale of alcoholic beverages. By 1907, Massachusetts had 250 dry towns and 100 wet towns. Maynard was wet; Concord, Acton and Stow were dry. The Friday evening trolley runs to Maynard were packed with families coming to shop, dine, perhaps see a movie or go to a dance hall, but before leaving town, the men would fill suitcases with hard liquor for the week back home.

Trolleys ran every thirty minutes from 6:00 a.m. to 11:00 p.m. End to end, it took sixty minutes. Patronage was consistently 1.0 to 1.2 million per year from 1902 through 1916, and the trolleys were profitable. After 1916, the business was not as good, and in later years, it was actually subsidized by the towns. With the car barn burning it 1918 (it was rebuilt), coal shortages due to the world war, deterioration of the rails and wires and rising competition from cars and buses, the system was in decline. The last run was January 16, 1923.

The trolley barn became the base for the Lovell Bus Lines, which operated from 1924 to 1954. Currently, it is an office complex. The power station next door became the St. Casimir Roman Catholic Church; currently St. Mary's Indian Orthodox Church. Most of the information for this section is from a book at the Maynard Public Library called *Concord, Maynard & Hudson Street Railway*.

WHEN HORSES ROAMED MAYNARD

Once upon a time Maynard was home to many horses. For example, in 1899 there were 256 horses. How is this known? Maynard's Annual Town Reports, on file at the Maynard Public Library, include Assessors' Reports that, from 1890 to 1933, included a horse tally for tax purposes.

A wealthy family of the precar era might have a carriage house on the property and keep a horse on site or board a horse at a livery stable in town. Richard Parmenter operated a stable off Concord Road. The site of the Fine Arts Theatre was once a livery stable. Maynard was also home to a number of urban barns. These were not remnants of working farms but rather one-horse barns for people who carted goods about town or to and from the railroad. Larger operations such as Parmenter Farm on the north edge of town were feeding and caring for dozens of horses for various businesses.

After 1899, the horse population declined, even though the number of dwellings on the assessors' records increased. In 1899, there were about 4 horses for every 10 dwellings on the assessor's records, or to be exact, 256 horses for 623 dwellings. Ten years later, it was 2 for every 10, and by 1919, there were only 123 horses for 1,205 dwellings. By the time the horse counting stopped in 1933, there were fewer than 20 horses living in Maynard. But even as late as the 1950s, there were still a few horses about town. Peter Grigas reminisced about how he and his friends rode their family-owned horses from Maynard to Stow on summer days, stopping at Erikson's Ice Cream on the way back.

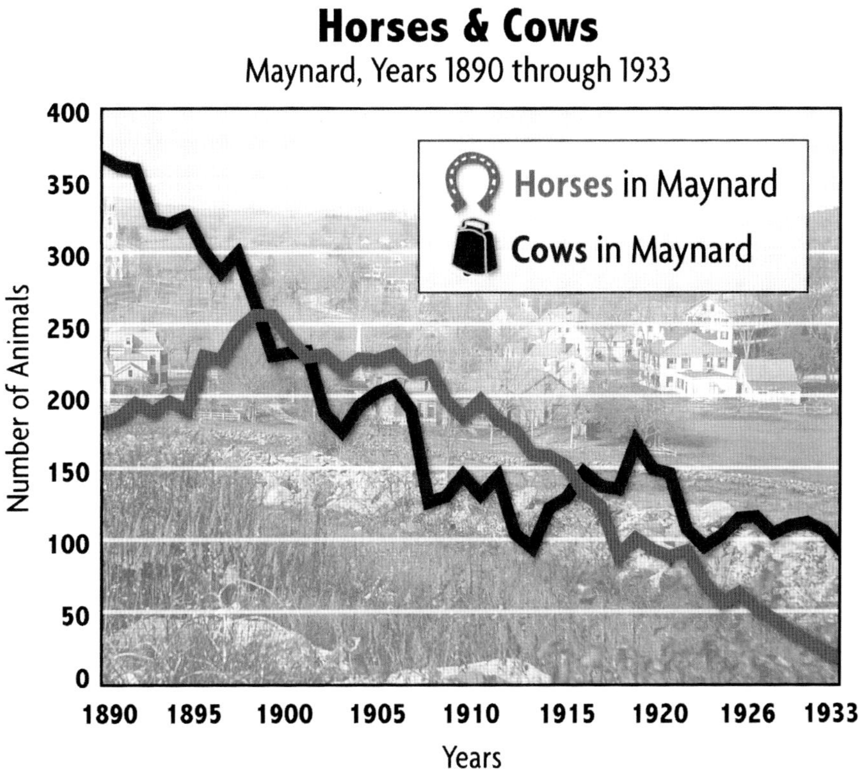

Proportionally, the drop in horse ownership was actually steeper than apparent from the chart, as the number of households doubled from 1900 to 1920, while horses declined from 256 to 120. The horse and cow count as of 2011 was zero. *Created by Felice Katz.*

Maynard was also a cow town. Records show that more than 350 milk cows resided in Maynard in 1890 and more than 100 as late as 1933. The records show an actual increase from 1914 to 1919, perhaps reflecting higher demand during World War I. Milk not used by local dairies might have been loaded onto an early morning "milk train" for transport elsewhere.

Living amid manure was the downside of life in Maynard. That peak number of horses would generate about four tons of manure daily, plus an additional two to three tons of urine, mostly at the stables but a fair bit on the roads. Unlike today's dog owners, horse owners did not feel obliged to clean up after their animals. The cows would have added another ton of manure, albeit not scattered about town but still contributing to the olfactory ambiance. And don't even start to think about the hundreds of pigs! Maynard was a horse town, a cow town, a pig town and a fly town!

The decline of the horse era had many causes. Key bicycle design improvements in the 1890s made bicycling tremendously popular, especially among women, who took to wearing "bloomers," after inventor Amelia Bloomer, rather than corsets and ankle-length skirts. Every town had its own bicycle club. The first car appeared in Maynard in 1899; the local electric trolley started operations in 1901. Mass production of cars, using methods transferred over from bicycle manufacturing by innovators such as Ransom Olds and later perfected by Henry Ford for the Model T, drove prices down. About the time of World War I, truck and tractor technology improved to the point that freight hauling and farming could be managed without horses. Today's Maynard has barns scattered here and there—a smattering of chickens, goats and alpacas—but no horses or cows.

FINNISH PUBLIC SAUNAS

The first syllable of "sauna" rhymes with "pow," hence "sow-na," with the accent on the first syllable. Taking a sauna means alternating between the heat of the sauna and the cold of a cold shower, perhaps rolling around outside in snow or, for the hardcore, jumping through a hole chopped into the ice of a frozen-over lake. "Avanto" is the hole chopped in ice, and "avantouinti" is the practice of ice swimming.

The sauna experience starts with dry heat, typically in the range of 140 to 194 degrees Fahrenheit but over 200 degrees for extremists. Humidity is less than 10 percent. Dry air is a poor conductor of heat. This is why sauna temperatures can be so high, while hot tubs are limited to 104

This wood-carved plaque inside a sauna depicts Mom washing Daughter in a tub while two family members on the high bench flail their backs with birch branches.

degrees, and the temperature in a 100 percent humidity steam bath is limited to 110 to 116 degrees.

"Löyly" may be beyond pronunciation by anyone not Finnish. Löyly is the heart of sauna. When water is thrown on superheated stones, the water is instantly converted to steam, which then condenses on cooler surfaces, such as skin. Just as evaporation cools, condensation and moisture on skin transfer heat. Thus, löyly is the intense wave of heat experienced about thirty seconds after water hits hot stones.

One hundred years ago, immigrants from Finland were the second most numerous immigrants in Maynard after the Irish, outnumbering those from Poland, Italy and Russia. Perhaps as much as 20 percent of Maynard's population was Finnish, as evidenced by names on many of the tombstones in Glendale Cemetery. Much like the earlier Irish immigration, which was triggered by very bad times (look up the Irish Potato Famine), Finns left their homeland for a reason. In their case, it accelerated during a period of Russification under Tsars Alexander III and Nicholas II. The Language Manifesto of 1900 made Russian the official language of Finland, and the conscription law of 1901 required all men of Finland to serve in the Russian Imperial Army.

Unsettled times continued through the Finnish Civil War of 1918, which resulted in deaths proportionate to what the United States suffered during our Civil War. Estimates are that more than 400,000 Finns came to the United States or Canada during the years 1860 to 1930. The first wave headed to Michigan and Minnesota, but later waves—more likely to be political refugees—also went to factory towns in New England. Russification, oppression, unrest and war were also catalysts for many Poles and Jews to come to America.

The largest concentration of immigrant Finns in Massachusetts were in Fitchburg and Worcester, with other groups in Maynard, Gardner, Quincy and Cape Ann. Maynard's Finnish immigrants started their own churches, co-operative associations, music bands and temperance societies, and built commercial saunas. Roy Helander, vice-president of Maynard's Historical Society, noted, "My father came over in 1903, my mother in 1909. They met in Maynard. My father worked as a weaver and foreman for the American Woolen Company until it closed in 1950."

Helander provided a tour of the sites of Maynard's former public sauna and/or steam bath buildings. The last ceased operating in the 1970s, but three of the buildings, now converted to other use, survive today. The sites were on Riverbank Road across from Town Hall, River Street, Florida Road north of the river, Elmwood Street and Powdermill Road. Maynard's Finnish immigrants also built saunas in their back yards. Classically, the private sauna building is small, maybe ten to twenty feet, has a chimney and is divided into two rooms. The first is for undressing. The second contains the stove and a tier of benches. In lieu of a lake, there should be a place to step out for a cold shower.

For more on sauna, read Michael Nordskog's book, *The Opposite of Cold*; it contains great descriptions of modern and traditional saunas, along with dozens of pictures.

ERIKSON'S ICE CREAM

After the floods of March 2010, the banks of the Assabet River yielded bucketsful of broken glass from beer bottles, medicine bottles, soda bottles and liquor bottles, plus one unbroken bottle that read "HALF PINT LIQUID, HANS ERIKSEN, MAYNARD, MASS." This find begged the question: was there any connection to Erikson's Ice Cream? Learning the answer helped date the bottle and, in the process, yielded a history that began with Hans Eriksen starting a dairy in Stow in 1902 and ends with the fifth generation of the family at Erikson's Ice Cream over one hundred years later.

Erikson's flavor specials for 2011 included Bear Claw and Brownie Batter.

Family records have Hans Eriksen starting a dairy farm and milk delivery business in Stow along White Pond Road. Home delivery was by horse and wagon. His son, Hans Eriksen Jr., returned from serving in the U.S. Army in France during World War I and took up the family business, which by this time had shifted to buying milk from local farmers rather than milking their own cows. Hans married Mary Boyd, assistant principal at Hale High School in Stow, in 1923.

Eriksen Jr. moved the dairy to its present site, just inside Maynard's border, in 1937 and started the ice cream operation next door, making 2011 the seventy-fourth year in the ice cream business. Back then, cream came from Buttericks Farm in Arlington, and flavoring ingredients were purchased from H.A. Johnson Company.

Hans Eriksen Sr. passed away in 1949. After the war ended but before his death, his son changed the family name and business name to "Erikson." Thus, the half-pint bottle found in the river was dated to between the move and Hans Sr.'s death.

Erikson Jr. continued the dairy bottling, delivery and ice cream businesses until he retired in 1961, with increasing help over time from his daughter, Arlene, and her husband, Joe Fraser. Once Arlene and Joe took over, they reorganized the business as Erikson Dairy, Inc. Within a few years, they sold the milk delivery routes to the United Cooperative Society of Maynard and then got out of milk processing entirely, retaining only the ice cream–related operations. About the same time, Hans's first cousin, Henry Erikson, was turning part of his farm property off Boxboro Road into an airstrip originally known as Erikson Field but now known as Minute Man Air Field.

The next generation of Frasers now manages the business, and their children—the fifth generation—have put in time scooping ice cream. Over the years, Erikson's has provided employment to thousands of high school students from Maynard, Stow and surrounding towns. Many of the alumni make a point of stopping in at Erikson's when visiting family or old friends still living in the area. Older alumni might be surprised to learn that Erikson's now offers hot dogs, soft-serve ice cream, nondairy options, plus souvenir T-shirts identical to staff wear.

Each season introduces unique flavors in addition to the large list of standards. Recent years' offerings included Freedom of Expresso and Green Monsta. Its location is on Route 117 on the west edge of Maynard, just before the Stow border. Credit cards are not accepted. Parking on the gravel/dirt is chaotic. Most visitors stand or retreat to their cars, but there are a few tables behind the building. Remember to look at the historic photos above the order windows.

And what was the fate of the river-rescued bottle? It was presented to the Fraser family as a memento.

Chapter 9

PLANTS

The wild spaces in Maynard and surrounding towns are now home to so many non-native species that we may be confused about which are native, which are well-behaved immigrants and which are ecologically destructive. Plus, some of the natives can be downright unfriendly. Every walk in the woods is enhanced by knowing names of what you see. For those nasty invasives, bring a folding saw.

BITTERSWEET

Invasive Species of the Year

Oriental bittersweet is a slow-motion disaster for the trees of New England. This ornamental plant "gone wild" was introduced to the United States in the mid-nineteenth century and widely naturalized by the early twentieth. When fully grown, it can overtop sixty foot tall trees, breaking branches with its weight and, finally, killing the trees.

Infestations of bittersweet are easiest to see in the winter, when the red berries are a colorful haze across bare treetops. In spring the berries are consumed by birds, contributing to the spread. Bittersweet likes full sunlight. It tends to grow fastest on trees bordering roads and open spaces. Growth rates are five to ten feet per year. Stems up to an inch or so in diameter are smooth with increasing roughness, as mature stems thicken to three to four inches in diameter. These vines are easy to differentiate from other vines. Poison ivy clings to the bark of the trees with thousands of fuzzy rootlets and rarely exceeds fifteen feet in height. Wild grape vines have a brown, flaking bark.

Combating bittersweet is both a private and public virtue. Property owners can begin by policing their own property. Vines should be cut as close to the ground as possible and also as high up as possible. The gap makes it harder for the new shoots to reach the old vine ends and get back into the trees. In time, what is left in the tree will rot and fall. For those who complain that the vines will just grow back, so does grass—but you commit to cutting that twice a month. Hardware stores should have products that can be applied with a brush across the cut stems to block regrowth. Small vines can be pulled up, roots and all. The roots are identified by a reddish-orange color. Just take care that you are not pulling up poison ivy, which can also be a ground-based, woody-stemmed plant.

Volunteer-minded individuals could approach their towns' conservation commissions for guidance on addressing bittersweet problems. The Friends

Volunteers cut bittersweet vines on Summer Hill. By ring count, some of these vines were twenty to thirty years old.

of the Assabet River National Wildlife Refuge periodically schedule work events to combat invasive plant species in the Refuge.

Invasive species are noteworthy based on how much they disrupt the ecological balance of their new land. Various world lists of the one hundred worst invasive species are not limited to plants. Insects populate the lists, as do mollusks, crabs, birds, reptiles (such as Burmese pythons in Florida) and even a smattering of mammals such as pigs, goats, cats and rats. Our international travels and trade continue to promote accidental or intentional introduction of species. An outbreak of Asian long-horned beetles is being combated in Worcester. In 2009, an outbreak of zebra mussels was found in Laurel Lake in the Berkshires. A year later, a "late blight" fungal infection damaged many of the tomato plants bought for home vegetable gardens.

Poison Ivy

Australia has many native poisonous plants but not poison ivy, nor does Asia, Africa, Europe or South America—just us. Poison ivy is native to almost all of mainland United States, with some boundary crossing into Canada and Mexico. England's affliction dates to colonial-era gardeners bringing it back to the old country as a decorative vine. As carbon dioxide increases in the atmosphere as part of global warming, poison ivy grows faster and more poisonous.

What exactly is poisonous about poison ivy? Leaves, stems, berries and roots contain an oily chemical compound called urushiol. This small molecule attaches itself to proteins in skin. Once attached, the body's immune system perceives the combination as a foreign invader. The resultant rash and intense itching are overreactions of the immune system, which typically take a day or so to appear. There is a window of opportunity of thirty minutes or so to wash off urushiol with soap and water before it binds. Adhering is irreversible: once it has attached, it cannot be transferred to another person or another part of the body. Not everyone is equally sensitive, with approximately 20 percent of people being resistant and an equal number being hypersensitive. People who are resistant can become sensitive over time and vice versa. Finally, urushiol is very stable, so tools, clothing and work gloves that come into contact with poison ivy can remain dangerous for months to years. An example is a hiker who laced up hiking boots in midsummer who ended up with itchy

Poison ivy is pervasive across New England.

hands because last summer she had walked through poison ivy. Animals don't get poison ivy. But if your dog romps through the woods, and you then pet your dog—whamo!

Poison ivy prefers partial shade, so it grows under shrubs, the edges of forests and along trails. One "pick-your-own" blueberry farm in eastern Pennsylvania was known to locals to not clear out the poison ivy from the blueberry bushes. That was just mean! The signature identification is clusters of three leaves with a smooth surface. In April, the emerging leaves are reddish and very shiny and, in fact, look similar to the emerging leaves on maple tree seedlings. Leaves lose shine as summer progresses, then turn red in the fall. As ground cover, poison ivy has woody stems up to twenty inches tall. As a vine, look for stems up to inches thick attached to tree trunks or other rough surfaces by hairy-looking rootlets. Oriental Bittersweet, in contrast, spirals up trees and has no clinging rootlets. In late fall, poison ivy berries will change from green to ivory colored, then remain on the plants all winter.

Roundup and other herbicides can be used to kill poison ivy. Follow the product's instructions. Remember that dead poison ivy plants still contain urushiol. Using a Weedwacker or lawn mower on poison ivy is a bad idea, as the aerosol of microfine droplets and plant fragments will affect skin and perhaps lungs. Worse is burning. Urushiol ends up in the smoke and can lead to skin, eye and lung irritation.

The extent of poison ivy on trails in Maynard and neighboring towns ranges from zero to severe. Even where it has been cleared, as on Maynard's portion of the Assabet River Rail Trail, stuff grows back. For a poison ivy–free experience, your prime hiking season is November to March—or you can stay on pavement or, better yet, leave the country. Numerous websites contain information about poison ivy. One, www.poison-ivy.org, has a color photo gallery skin rash hall of fame.

Skunk Cabbage

Two signs of spring occur in early April: hand-sized skunk cabbage leaves and young men starting to drive their convertibles with the top down. Both push the season. Compared to skunk cabbages, all other woodland plants are just beginning to show leaf buds, and women are not yet driving convertibles. Let's focus today on the botanical story and leave the human mystery to the social psychologists.

The Latinate nomenclature for skunk cabbage, *Symplocarpus foetidus*, makes clear this plant stinks. Tearing or crushing leaves will release a sulfurous smell akin to a whiff of skunk, combined with notes of rotten eggs, garlic and rotting flesh—more on this later.

Skunk cabbage prefers boggy woodlands. In midsummer, these regions will be dry and in deep shade, but at the front end of spring they are wet from snowmelt and are sunlit. During April the leaves are unfurling, growing and, in time, forming plants that will be two to four feet across. Each stalk ends in one leaf. At full growth the leaves superficially resemble the open leaves surrounding a head of cabbage, hence the name. By mid-July, when the trees are full of leaves, skunk cabbage leaves are already beginning to decay. By mid-August, all that is left are root clusters under the soil's surface, waiting for next year.

The unfurling of green leaves is actually a skunk cabbage's second act. Weeks earlier, a specialized leaf called a spathe emerged from the ground. Spathes are not green. Instead, their colors are positively Lovecraftian: eggplant-like purples, wine-dark maroons, streaked or mottled with yellowish green. As far as size, spathes are three to six inches tall. For its shape, think

Skunk cabbage is related to jack-in-the-pulpit and calla lily.

of a somewhat stretched Hershey's Kiss, three inches across at the base, with the top twisted and/or tipped to one side. Inside the spathe and accessible to the outside by only a narrow opening, a stalk forms with a flower head atop, called a spadix. Carrion-feeding flies enticed by the rotting smell enter the spathe space, pick up pollen in the process of exploring the spadix, then depart to visit other spathes, completing the fertilization process.

Skunk cabbages have one trick shared with just a few other plant species: heat generation. The air space inside the spathe will be fifteen to thirty degrees higher than the outside temperatures. Heat protects the flower from freezing, plus the combination of warmth and odor attracts the flies that will be fooled into the task of fertilization.

Chapter 10

Striving

Ask any outdoor adventuring athlete in New England for a hardship story and you will hear tales of dehydration, hypothermia, hyperthermia and overhydration. Or don't ask, and you will hear the same.

Hypothermia, or "Aren't you cold?"

To see teenage males at a school bus stop on a winter morning, dressed in no more than shorts and a hoodie, is to believe that some magical cold proofing has been discovered. One wants to ask, "Aren't you cold? Does your mother know you are out in that?" On both counts, apparently not.

Perhaps what the boys are demonstrating is the distinction between feeling cold and being cold. Men of a tender age tend to have a low percent body fat compared to girls, say 10 to 15 percent compared to 18 to 22 percent. Part of the difference is boys having less subcutaneous (under the skin) fat. This means boys will have better blood circulation to and from skin. Also, underlying muscle will be closer to the skin. Both differences warm skin at the expense of lowering core body temperature faster. The end result is girls feel cold faster than boys. In a similar fashion, alcohol relaxes surface blood vessels, so drinkers feel the cold less, while at the same time, they are losing heat faster.

The distinction between sensing cold on skin and losing core body temperature is important to anyone planning outdoor activities, ranging

Vigorous exercise can mask the onset of hypothermia.

from walking, biking and water sports (winter sailboat racing, anyone?) to skiing, ice fishing and snowmobiling. Exposed skin is prone to frostbite in very cold weather, especially when moving fast or exposed to strong winds. At temperatures above freezing, the frostbite risk is gone, but hypothermia still occurs at temperatures well into the fifties.

Shivering sets in once core body temperature drops below ninety-five degrees. Shivering—i.e., involuntary muscle twitching—burns fuel to generate heat. When muscle cells contract, more than half the energy used is "wasted" on heat production rather than contraction. In cool weather, bumblebees prewarm their flight muscles via shivering. As core temperatures head toward ninety degrees, our shivering response becomes stronger and the "umbles" set in, as in having the fumbles, stumbles, grumbles and mumbles. Emergency medical treatment is warranted when temperatures fall below ninety degrees.

Paradoxically, vigorous exercise in cold weather increases risk of hypothermia and thus can be described as an exercise trap. First, exercise blunts perception of cold. A university study of people exposed to cold and either exercising or not exercising found that the ones who were exercising "felt" less cold even though their core and surface temperatures were declining at the same rate as when not exercising. Movement contributes to wind chill. Exercise also generates heat and sweat. Sweat, just like rain or immersion in water, reduces the insulating quality of protective clothing. Finally, prolonged endurance exercise can result in depletion of muscle fuel and either delay or compromise the shivering response.

In the United States, hypothermia accounts for about seven hundred deaths per year. That figure includes deaths due to alcohol-related exposure and homelessness but not boating accidents in cold water, which are instead logged as drowning. Wooded areas of even fairly well-developed Massachusetts towns are large enough to get into trouble in cold weather. At the practical level, don't go out alone, especially in the fast-fading light of late afternoon. If heading out alone, someone should know where you intend to be and when you expect to return. A cellphone doubles as a means to call for help and a GPS device, aiding emergency rescue to home in on your location.

Getting back to our teenage boys, deliberately underdressing for cold weather may be a form of preening for members of the opposite sex. Males of many species demonstrate their superior fitness by growing the largest horns or the brightest feathers or showing physical prowess over other males. Being apparently impervious to cold is one more way of claiming to be a physically prime specimen of manhood. Is it also demonstrating mental superiority? Not so much.

Avoiding Overhydration and Hyponatremia

Every year more than one million people participate in marathons and other endurance events. The hydration dogma for endurance athletes is "drink before you are thirsty." The dogma is wrong and potentially dangerous.

With today's cult of hydration, 5 to 20 percent of people completing endurance events such as a marathon, triathlon, cross-country skiing event or a one-hundred-mile bicycle ride will weigh more at the end than when they started. Studies have shown that when athletes drink to satisfy thirst they tend to replace about 75 percent of the water they are losing during the endurance event. This, rather than consciously drinking to not lose any weight, appears to be the safer target. Losing up to 2 percent of pre-event weight during the event does not appear to affect

Drinking BOLD, COLD or OLD water—or even sports beverages—during a lengthy endurance event to the point that you weigh more at the end of the event than at the beginning can result in low blood sodium concentrations and serious symptoms, from headache up to confusion, stupor, seizures, coma and even death. *Drawing by Louis D'Amico.*

performance. Full recovery from the mild event-related dehydration can take place after the event is over.

The health risk from overhydration is that it lowers sodium concentration in the blood, resulting in a condition called hyponatremia. From one review of 2,135 endurance race athletes, 10 percent had gained weight by the end of their event, 3 percent had blood sodium below the normal range and 1 percent had symptoms associated with low sodium, which causes cells to retain water, resulting in swelling.

While puffy ankles are not a serious health problem, swelling of the brain is. The brain is encased in a rigid container—the skull—and cannot expand. From mild to severe, the signs and symptoms of overhydration can include one or more of the following: headache; nausea; puffiness of the face, ankles and hands; dizziness; confusion; agitation; vomiting; respiratory distress; stupor; coma; seizures; and, very rarely, death.

There is a belief that drinking sports drinks instead of water will replace electrolytes (sodium, potassium and magnesium) lost from sweating. These beverages do not contain enough sodium to replace loss. If consumed in excess, hyponatremia can result.

Contributing to the incidence of overhydration is the fact that, for some people, prolonged exercise turns off urine production even if they are adequately hydrated and are not in a low-sodium state. These are the people who can complete a four-hour marathon or a seven-hour bike century without needing to use the Port-O-Potty. The effect can continue for hours after exercise stopped. Thinking that "no pee" means dehydration, these people continue drinking water, sports drinks and other beverages—beer—in an attempt to trigger urine production. The best protection is to check postevent weight against pre-event weight and not drink any more fluids if already heavier afterward compared to before.

The International Marathon Medical Directors Association (IMMDA) recommends athletes drink to satisfy thirst. The IMMDA also recommends that for marathon participants, any weight gain constitutes justification for a medical consultation. The same thinking would apply to bicyclists and triathlon competitors.

Women are at higher risk for hyponatremia than men, as are smaller-bodied athletes compared to larger. Cooler weather increases risk, as it inhibits sweating. Chronic aspirin or other NSAIDS use may increase risk.

All this is not to say that dehydration is not the more common risk. That same large study reporting 3 percent as being overhydrated found that 50 percent were dehydrated, which was defined in the study as having lost more than 3 percent of pre-event body weight. Under warm, dry conditions, an exercising athlete can lose a quart, equal to two pounds, of water per hour. Again, weighing oneself with an accurate digital scale before and after training sessions is a good means to learning how to achieve water balance.

For the hypochondriacs wanting to look up everything on the Internet, exercise-associated hyponatremic encephalopathy (EAHE) is the term for when hyponatremia causes swelling of the brain. Syndrome of inappropriate antidiuretic hormone secretion (SIADH) refers to postexercise suppression of urine production.

Recovery After Donating Blood

Spring is when many local endurance athletes start increasing training for events such as marathons and one-hundred-mile bicycle rides. These athletes may hesitate to donate blood because they worry about compromising subsequent performance. The volume collected is five hundred milliliters (about a pint) in most countries, with standard postdonation instructions not to exercise or do manual labor for a day or two and to not donate again for fifty-six days. Recent research shines a light on the complicated timing of recovery from a blood donation.

The first thing to know is that men average 8 percent blood by weight; women, 6 percent. The largest part of the difference is due to women having about 25 percent more body fat compared to men of the same athletic fitness. Age can also affect the initial impact of donating blood. As people age, there is a trend for the amount of blood-rich muscle to decrease and for the amount of blood-poor fat to increase. The net result is that a donation will have a different initial impact based on sex, size, age and physical fitness of the donor. For example, a donation will be a much larger percent of total blood volume for a small, middle-aged, sedentary woman than it will for a large, young, athletic man.

Second thing to know is that taking an iron supplement or eating iron-rich foods will not speed recovery. With the exception of people who are iron deficient, there are adequate reserves of iron in the form of ferritin, an iron-rich protein, to replace what was removed. The rate-limiting factor is how fast bone marrow can increase red blood cell production over the normal replacement rate.

A research article published in 2008 gives a picture of the donation recovery process in healthy young men. Dr. Torben Pottgiesser removed 550 milliliters of blood from twenty-nine men and then measured plasma and total body hemoglobin twice a week. Plasma, the fluid part of blood, recovered within one to three days. This fast recovery of fluid volume is what most people think is all that affects exercise capacity. But plasma does not carry oxygen.

Hemoglobin, in red blood cells, is the protein responsible for transporting oxygen. In these men, hemoglobin did not even begin to recover in the first five to ten days. It took, on average, thirty-six days for the subjects' hemoglobin to return to the levels seen before the blood donation. The full range was twenty to fifty-nine days, with 25 percent having recovered by twenty-five days, 50 percent by thirty-four days and 75 percent by forty-six days. Thus, for these young men, the results support the standard practice of having donors wait at least fifty-six days before donating blood again. The equivalent experiments have not yet been published for women or older donors.

In theory, at anything up to moderately vigorous exercise there will be no difference in perceived exercise capacity. The heart will beat faster to compensate for less oxygen-carrying capacity per heart beat; however, the high end will be compromised. Amateur cyclists were tested before and after a blood donation. At seven days, donated hemoglobin was down 6.7 percent, and maximum exercise as measured in watts output was down 7.1 percent. Unfortunately, no testing was conducted beyond seven days.

On a practical note, anyone planning to compete in a long-distance endurance event should not schedule a blood donation during the final eight weeks leading up to the event. Training can resume within a few days after the donation with the understanding that training performance will likely be compromised for weeks.

Snowshoes

Start with the classic nightmare of running from danger in foot-dragging slow motion. Add winter cold and lots of snow and—voila—you are snowshoeing. The conundrum of snowshoe ownership in this part of Massachusetts is that it rarely snows enough to justify owning snowshoes. When it does, snowshoeing is hard, slow work. On dry land, very good runners can maintain ten to twelve miles per hour for long distances. Cross-country skiers are even faster. In contrast, for snowshoe racing five to six miles per hour is considered a good speed. For the plodder who walks at three to four miles per hour, a speed of two miles per hour is realistic, but it will require far more calories per hour than walking, especially if punching through the crust with each step and needing to lift out before stepping forward.

So, why snowshoe? First, it is meditative in a way that a gym's treadmill is not. Nature is pared to the essentials. On the morning after a night storm, the snow is a painter's palette of whites. Plant life is all dark limbs draped in white. The sky is shades of gray. The only sound is your footsteps, and when

According to meteorological records, precipitation totals for eastern Massachusetts have gradually increased over the last one hundred years. Of the ten snowiest winters on record since 1890, five have been in the last twenty years. Time to buy snowshoes!

you stop, there is silence or perhaps the distant honking of a flock of geese out looking for breakfast.

Subsequent morning walks will find many signs of life. Deer, coyote, rabbit, squirrel and all the other nonhibernating mammals will be about, looking for food and water. One benefit of snowshoes is the ease of going off-trail to follow tracks or look for signs. In the evergreens, squirrels and birds feeding on buds and pine cone seeds will produce a shower of detritus under the trees. Berry-feeding birds will leave colorful markers under their roost trees. Field mice leave a trail of jump marks four to eight inches apart with the faint mark of a dragging tail behind each hop.

Snowshoes are designed for intended use: recreational, hiking, back country or racing. The science of snow dictates a burden of roughly three-fourths pounds per square inch of shoe surface for powdery snow—less for firm or packed snow. This translates to snowshoes twenty to thirty-six inches long and eight to ten inches wide, depending on user weight and intended use. Brands available locally include Tubbs, Atlas, MSR and TSL. Prices for adult shoes will range from $100 to $300. Variables include ease of getting the snowshoes on/off, types of boots they will accommodate, grip, weight and so on. Tubbs alone has ten adult models. So unless you are already an expert, shopping at a store with knowledgeable sales staff is a plus. Necessary accessories are adjustable length walking poles for $50 to $100. Assortments of layered and vented clothing will keep you warm when not moving but will not retain sweat moisture when you are trekking.

Paved rail trails such as ARRT (Hudson), Bruce Freedman (Chelmsford), Nashua River (Ayer) or Minuteman (Bedford) offer venues twelve feet wide, no steep climbs and no motorized vehicles mucking up the snow. Maps for these and more can be found by using the "find a trail" function at www.traillink.com. Towns may get around to snowplowing trail parking lots but will not plow the trails. Most town forests have miles of woodland trails, as does the Assabet River National Wildlife Refuge. But stay off golf courses and farm fields. As appealing as they look, trespassing is trespassing. And keep in mind that a level area with no plant growth visible above the snow is probably a pond, not a field. Yes, now you can walk on snow; no, you cannot walk on water.

Chapter 11

Marble/Whitney/Parmenter Farm

Who knew a hole in the ground could have such a long history? There are ties to the Salem witch trials and a connection to Richard Whitney; his wife, Hannah; and his other wife, Hannah. This site on the north edge of Maynard is referred to on various maps as "Marble Farm," "Whitney Farm" or "Parmenter Crossing," but in actuality, those names represent six generations of one family living at the site for more than two hundred years. Add years from their immigration to the colonies at one end to the years after the house burned in 1924 at the other, and you have one family history spanning nearly four hundred years.

Last Names

In the sixteenth century, European governments started insisting that people take last names for purposes of tax collection and census taking. These names could be based on location, occupation or perhaps a personal characteristic. "Marble" was a name for people who lived near Marble Hill in Cheshire, England and perhaps, at the same time, an occupational name for craftsmen who worked with marble. Whitney was a location name taken from the old English "hwit" for white and "ey" for water and perhaps referred to the whitewater rapids on the River Wye that run through Whitney in Herefordshire. Parmenter was a French-derived occupational name, "Parmentier" being a term for a maker of decorative trimmings and facings for clothing. John Parmenter, our immigrant, was a tailor in England.

THE GREAT MIGRATION AND KING PHILIP'S WAR

John Marble, John Whitney and John Parmenter, along with their wives and children, all immigrated to America as part of the English Great Migration. Puritans opposed the practices of the Church of England. In the 1620s, the Puritan-supported political party gained control of Parliament. In reaction, King Charles I dissolved Parliament in 1629 and assumed absolute rule. Puritans were oppressed by the king, but the king also approved the Massachusetts Bay Charter, giving Puritans the right to establish a colony in the region of the New World where the *Mayflower* had landed. During the years 1630 to 1640, more than twenty thousand Puritans made the voyage. Unlike many immigrant movements in which the men voyage first and then send for spouses and families if successful, the Puritans traveled mostly as families. They were skilled craftsmen and farmers. Some were wealthy and brought servants. In 1641, England's Civil War started between the Puritans and the king, which led to the execution of King Charles I and Oliver Cromwell assuming rule in 1651. The Puritan immigration fell to a trickle once the war started—and, in fact, some returned to fight in the war, but there was enough of a critical mass for the New England colonies to succeed.

King Philip's War (1675–1676), also known at Metacom's War, set the Wampanoag, Nipmuc and Narragansett tribes against the English colonists. King Philip/Metacom was the son of Massasoit, the Wampanoag chief who had been on good terms with the *Mayflower* Pilgrims and helped them survive their first winter of 1620–1621. Metacom saw the Indians progressively displaced. He is quoted as stating, "I am determined not to live until I have no country." More than half of the ninety towns in New England came under attack. Lore has it that Indians met on Pomposattakutt Hill, now Summer Hill, to decide whether to attack Concord or Sudbury. The answer: Sudbury. Any early settlers in what is now Stow and Maynard were killed, kidnapped or driven off, with their homes and barns destroyed.

The Mohegan, Poduck and "Praying Indian" tribes aided the colonists. But the Indians who sided with the colonists also suffered hardships. Some were temporarily relocated to Deer Island in Boston Harbor with inadequate food and shelter. Many died during the winter. England's government under King Charles II did little to aid the colonists during this struggle. Only after the war did colonial settlers return.

Marble Family

The model for colonial expansion was for existing towns to establish new clusters of homes and cleared farm and pasture land five to ten miles away as "plantations." Pomposattakutt Plantation was an intended 1669 spin-off settlement from Sudbury, as Acton was from Concord. In 1683, after resettlement after Metacom's War, the territory was incorporated as the town of Stow.

John and Judith Marble arrived in 1635, perhaps on the ship *Jonathan*. Their son, Joseph, moved to Andover. All of Joseph Marble's children were born in Andover, the last one in 1691. Joseph bought 165 acres of land in Sudbury in 1704. His son, Joseph Marble Jr., had a child born in Andover in 1707 and then his next child in Stow in 1713. Joseph's sons, John and Edmund, also married in Andover and later had children born in Stow. So it appears that a fairly large Marble clan moved to Stow in the early 1700s, either all at once or progressively as more land was cleared.

Confirmed as living on site are Joseph Marble (b. 1650); his son, John Marble (b. 1680), who married Abigail Merriam; their son, John Marble (b.

The John Marble interred in Maynard's Glendale Cemetery is the great-grandson of Joseph Marble, who bought the land in 1704.

1717), who married Rebekah Farnsworth; and John Marble (b. 1751), who married Lois Davis. John and Lois had four children, but their three sons died young. Sarah, their daughter, married Daniel Whitney, also of Stow. Sarah died in 1863, the last of the Marbles to live in the home. Daniel and Sarah were buried in Maynard's Glendale Cemetery in the same plot as Sarah's parents, John and Lois Marble.

Which town they lived in is a complex question. As noted, records show Joseph Marble buying land in Sudbury. There are records of him attending Sudbury town meetings. When Stow incorporated in 1683, a good-sized area of what is now northern Maynard had initially remained part of Sudbury. In 1730, Joseph's son, John, and his neighbors successfully petitioned to switch their land to being part of Stow. In 1871, the same land was included in the creation of Maynard. Thus, over the years, the homestead was located in three different towns: Sudbury until 1730; Stow, 1730–1871; and then Maynard, 1871 to present day.

The Faulkner Connection

The historic Faulkner Home in Acton is an example of a "named" home with a prior history. In 1702, three men signed agreements and contracts to develop land known as the Iron Work Farm. They built mills and homes flanking a dam on Fort Brook. This was the making of the area now known as South Acton. Ammi Ruhamah Faulkner rented the mills in 1738 and then purchased them in 1742. Ammi's name is interesting. "Ammi" and "Ruhamah" are derived from Hebrew and respectively mean "my people" and "have obtained mercy." That's an appropriate name for someone whose mother and two preteen sisters had been accused of being witches in the Salem and Andover witch trials of 1692–1693 and whose mother, Abigail Faulkner, of Andover, would have been executed if not pregnant with him at the time of her conviction.

Joseph Marble, who was married to Abigail's sister, posted bond in 1692 to have Abigail's daughters released from jail. The New England witch trials were a late and distant echo of the European witch hunts of 1480–1700 that had seen tens of thousands of people, mostly women, accused of witchery and executed. Fifty years after the Andover trials, Ammi's Marble cousins lived a mile south of his Acton home and likely had their corn ground at his gristmill and their logs cut to beams and boards at his timber mill. Six generations of Faulkners lived in the house over a 202-year period.

Whitney Family

The Whitney Museum in New York, Eli Whitney of the cotton gin, the Whitneys involved in Thoroughbred horse racing, the Whitney founder of the Mets baseball team, the Stow cemetery near Maynard that has a separate Whitney Gate to get to the section where many Whitneys are buried: why so many Whitneys? John Whitney and his wife, Elinor, came over in 1635 on the ship *Elizabeth and Anne* with four sons and had four more sons in New England. And those children had children, their children had children, and so on. The Whitney Research Group estimates that there are more than fifteen thousand descendents of John and Elinor Whitney.

John and Elinor Whitney were wealthy landowners in Watertown. Their son, Richard (1626–1697), is listed as still living in Watertown as of 1673 but later as "a proprietor" in Stow as of 1680. A cluster of Whitneys were buried in the Stow Lower Village Cemetery. Richard's son, Richard (1660–1723), is there next to his wife, Elizabeth. His son, Richard (1692–1775), is there next to his wife, Hannah. And next to Hannah is Richard's second wife, also Hannah. Richard and Hannah I had eight children before she died at the age of fifty. Two years later, he married Hannah II, a widow who had five children from her first marriage. Richard and Hannah II had no additional children. They both passed away in 1775 after thirty years together. Richard's son, Daniel (1720–1782), was buried nearby, as is his son, Daniel (1749–1805). But that Daniel's son, also named Daniel (1785–1870), was buried in Maynard along with his wife, Sarah Marble. There are Whitneys listed in local area phone books to this day.

Parmenter Family

John Parmenter, church deacon, came over with his wife, Bridget, and his son, John Parmenter Jr., in 1639; the ship's name unknown. Fresh off the boat, they moved to the Sudbury Plantation, a spin-off settlement from Watertown. John Parmenter Jr. and his wife, Amy, had six children. Through their daughter, Mary, one of the descendents was Samuel Morse, inventor of the telegraph.

The Parmenters were tavern owners in Sudbury. After a series of mundane names—John, John, George, George—twins born in 1709 were named Deliverance and Thankful. Perhaps it was a difficult birth? Deliverance's sons, Deliverance Jr. and Jason, fought in the Revolutionary War. Deliverance Jr. returned to Sudbury and married Mary Osborne, and the two of them had Nahum and eight other children. Our line of interest goes from Nahun to Joel Parmenter to Joel F. Parmenter.

Deliverance Jr.'s great-grandson, Joel F. Parmenter, was born in 1831. He married Mary L. Whitney in 1855. He bought his way out of the Civil War draft in 1863, a common practice at the time. He and Mary moved into the Marble/Whitney home in 1871 after Mary's father died.

Joel F. Parmenter's 1919 obituary in the *Maynard News* introduced some confusion into the family history. It stated that the Marble house "was built previous to 1683, and the land on which it stands was granted to the Marble family, who came over from England in the "Speedwell" around 1648." As noted earlier, the Marbles crossed the ocean in 1635. The *Speedwell* was supposed to be a companion ship to the *Mayflower* in 1620, but the only record of it ever reaching the colonies has it sailing in 1656. There is strong evidence that the Marble family was still in Andover into the late 1690s. The unsolved mysteries are who owned the land prior to Joseph Marble purchasing land in 1704 and whether a house belonging to a previous owner stood on the site prior to their arrival.

Last of the line in residence is Joel F. and Mary Parmenter and their five children. The four surviving at the time of their father's death—Daniel, Richard, J. Willis and Harry—were in their forties to sixties, and it appears that no one moved back into the house. Most of the Parmenter property and a half interest in the house were sold after Joel's death in 1919, probably to settle inheritances to his children and grandchildren. Harry, the youngest son, was half owner of the house at the time of the fire. He lived in Worcester. The other half was owned by Martin Peterson of Maynard. At the time of the fire, Harry's half was rented to Michael Taraswich and his family, and the other half was empty. The house was not rebuilt. In time, the land came to be owned by the town of Maynard, probably seized for nonpayment of taxes. Maynard's World War I Memorial shows Joel's grandsons, Joel F. and Daniel L. Parmenter, serving as privates in the U.S. Army. Parmenter Avenue and Parmenter Street, off of Concord Street, were probably named after Daniel Parmenter, who had a farm and livery business there. Richard Parmenter was described as being an overseer at the mill and living on Summer Street.

The House

There is a photo of the house, date unknown, in the Gutteridge book *A Brief History of Maynard*, published 1921. From the photo, it appears to have been in the Georgian Colonial style. The foundation paces off to approximately thirty-two by twenty-eight feet with the front facing south. The west side has a flight of stone stairs to the basement. The east side has an extension of the foundation that had supported bay windows on the first and second floors. The back right corner had an extension of the foundation to the north and an extension of stones past the foundation. This was likely the kitchen and servants' quarters, respectively. It is possible that the extension past the foundation was the original house. The large chimneys seen in the photo suggest that when built, the house was heated by wood-burning fireplaces in every room. The windows appear to be double hung. This innovation was introduced around 1700. Rusted iron window counterweights were found in the debris in the foundation.

According to the *Concord Enterprise*, the fire started the afternoon of April 2. Within one and a half hours, the house had collapsed into the foundation, all ablaze. The fire department had reached the fire in a timely fashion, but because the nearest fire hydrant was more than a quarter mile away, they could do nothing to save the house. *Courtesy of Maynard Historical Society.*

Georgian Colonial–style homes became popular in the colonies starting in 1700 and remained in vogue through the 1830s. The design incorporated a simple decorative crown above the centered door, with the door flanked on either side by two windows, five windows on the second floor and two chimneys. With decorative embellishments, it evolved into the Federal/Adams style.

Visible in the Gutteridge photo behind the Parmenter house is a large complex of barns. Joel F. Parmenter's obituary states that the oldest barn was marked with a 1722 date. The newspaper report on the fire of 1924 stated that the barn housed twenty-six horses at the time of the fire and was unharmed. It does not say who owned or operated the barn at the time of the fire, but Joel's son, Daniel Parmenter, owned a farm and livery off of Concord Road at the time of the 1920 federal census. The Maynard Assessor's Record of 1924 shows ninety-two horses.

THE PRESENT DAY

What the town of Maynard owns is a site where a farmhouse and outbuildings were built, possibly as early as the late 1600s, with one family living at the site for more than two hundred years. The site borders Rockland Avenue, off Acton Road where it meets Route 27. The house burned on April 2, 1924, leaving a debris-filled, stone-walled foundation. There are no visible traces of the large barns, which were to the west. The debris includes tons of broken chimney brick from when the two large chimneys collapsed during or after the fire. The foundation is either dry-laid or mortared fieldstone with a partial top layer of large, squared off granite blocks. The other parts of the top layer tumbled into the foundation and are part of the debris.

There are two wells and four sets of stone steps on the property. The most striking of the stone steps is on the west side of the foundation, leading from ground level down to the basement. Each of the eight steps is one piece of granite spanning four feet from wall to wall and weighing more than six hundred pounds. There are also sizeable stone walls framing the homesite and providing a border between the homesite and the future Assabet River Rail Trail.

On April 4, 2009, Maynard Boy Scout Troop 130 spent the better part of a damp spring day cutting down trees and clearing brush from the Marble Farm site and erecting a post and chain fence bordering two sides of the

Left: These granite steps to the basement were shaped and moved without power tools. When the 2009 cleanup began, the bottom half of the flight was buried under dirt, naturally composted from nearly a century of leaf fall.

Below: Maynard's Boy Scout Troop 130 and their fathers cleared the site on April 4, 2009, eighty-five years to the week from the date of the fire, as part of Jason Schomacker's Eagle Scout project. *Photo by John O'Buck.*

foundation. This was an Eagle Scout project by Jason Schomacker. A plaque on one of the fence posts shows a photo of the house taken before the fire, with barns and other outbuildings seen in the background. The site has the potential for being an interesting and easily accessible addition to Maynard's history, but without continuing maintenance, it gets rapidly overgrown with sumac, bittersweet, knotweed, bramble and poison ivy.

LIVING DESCENDENTS

Marble/Whitney/Parmenter Farm was the topic of a presentation given by Peg Brown and David Mark before the Maynard Historical Society in 2009. Attending were two descendents of Joseph Marble. Charles Marble of Boylston had recently moved to the area from Syracuse, New York, and knew no more than that his family had come from "somewhere around here." It was pure happenstance that someone asked him if he was related to the Marbles of the upcoming talk about Marble Farm. It turned out he was a direct descendent of Joseph's son, John Marble.

A plaque marks the site. The disputed 1683 date was taken from Gutteridge's 1921 *A Brief History of Maynard*.

Sally Wadman lives in Sudbury and knew that she descended from one of Joseph's other sons—Edmund Marble—but had had no idea where Edmund had lived. Sudbury town records have on file Edmund Marble marrying Mary Jewell in August 1711. Their daughter, Dorothy, married Moses Chandler in 1742, and through their son, Samuel Chandler, Sally was born eight generations later. "Chandler," derived from candle maker, is another New England name that dates its arrival to the early 1600s, in this case to a William Chandler who arrived around 1637. Through Sally's genealogical research, she is able to connect her grandchildren with Marble, Jewell and Chandler ancestors who all arrived within twenty years after the *Mayflower*.

Town records have Joseph transferring land to John and Edmund in 1726, so both brothers are placed as having lived at the farm. Edmund moved away; John stayed.

Charles Marble, Sally Wadman and their families have visited the homestead of their ancestors, taking away memories and photos. A useful resource for anyone researching Pilgrim-era immigration is http://www.packrat-pro.com/ships/shiplist.htm. This database of early ships is searchable by the passenger's name, the ship's name or the year of sailing.

Chapter 12

Twenty-First Century

A history as a nineteenth-century mill town has repercussions in the twenty-first century. Maynard's small houses on small property lots and higher percentage of rental properties—some of those dating back a century—have resulted in a higher population density compared to surrounding towns, lower median housing prices and lower median household incomes needed to afford those housing prices, all of which is shown in the table. The rising tide of young parents with young children, evidenced by the weekend flow of stroller pushers seen downtown, confirms Maynard's current niche as a starter-home community. According to 2010 data from www.city-data.com:

Town	**Area per Square Mile**	**Pop. (Est.)**	**Pop. per Square Mile**	**% Rentals**	**Median House Price**	**Median Income**
Maynard	5.2	10,100	1,942	30%	$308,000	$78,100
Acton	19.8	20,400	1,030	24	536,000	117,500
Concord	25.0	17,500	700	19	725,000	123,200
Sudbury	24.3	17,300	710	8	692,000	152,200
Stow	17.6	6,100	350	13	485,000	123,600

Assabet River Annual Cleanup

September 11, 2010, was the twenty-fourth annual cleanup of the Assabet River and its tributaries. Staff and volunteers from the Organization for the Assabet River (OAR) had previously searched the banks and bottoms of the watercourses for sites with the most trash. Each town had a 9:00 a.m. meeting to assign work. At 12:00 p.m., the tired, sweaty, muddy and perhaps slimy volunteers reassembled for pizza and beverages before going home for a well-deserved personal cleanup.

Cleanup tasks roughly divide into muckers, heavers and drylanders. Muckers work in the river, either wearing waterproof waders or old pants and shoes that they are willing to get very wet. Trash found in the river is loaded into canoes that serve as shallow draft barges to transport trash to the haul-out sites. Heavers work at the edge of the river. They remove trash from the canoes and either drag or heave it to the top of the riverbank. There, drylanders drag everything to the piles that will later be collected by the Department of Public Works trucks from the various towns. Drylanders also collect and bag trash that can be reached along the riverbanks without getting wet.

Tires are a perennial find, ditto to broken glass, beer cans and mysterious pieces of rusted steel. More unusual and harder to remove finds have included bus seats, a TV/stereo console, a dishwasher, a queen-sized mattress and box spring and a three-foot-tall safe from the York Safe and Lock Company, with the door partially torn off. York made safes in York, Pennsylvania, starting in 1883, until it was bought by Diebold in 1946. How and when this safe ended up in the river is anyone's imaginative guess.

Research has yet to show whether the Assabet was ever polluted enough to catch fire. Many industrialized rivers caught fire now and then. The Cuyahoga River in Cleveland famously caught fire in 1969. That was not the first or worst fire on the Cuyahoga. A fire in 1952 caused more than $1 million in damage. But the 1969 fire got huge press, echoed by the song "Burn On" released on Randy Newman's 1972 album *Sail Away*. The chorus was "Burn on, big river, burn on." Congress passed the Clean Water Act in 1972.

One visible gain from cleaning up the Assabet River is that progressively, over the years, less new trash ends up in the river. The "broken window theory," first in print in 1982, holds that vandalism is contagious—i.e., unrepaired vandalism triggers more vandalism—and perhaps more controversially, triggers an increase in more serious crimes. In theory, zero

Volunteers from the Organization for the Assabet, Sudbury and Concord Rivers have removed hundreds of car tires from the river over the years, along with bicycles, car parts and mysterious pieces of twisted metal. *Photo by David Griffin.*

tolerance for small crimes reduces the rate of large crimes. Whether true for criminal behavior, littering is clearly contagious; the more litter remains visible, the more likely people will litter.

OAR became OARS in 2011 to acknowledge an expansion to being the Organization for the Assabet, Sudbury and Concord Rivers. Anyone interested in participating in future river cleanups can call the OARS offices at 978-369-3956. In addition to the annual cleanup, OARS needs volunteers to conduct periodic water quality sampling and occasional efforts to combat invasive water plants.

Independent from the OARS cleanup, there is a National River Cleanup effort that was started around 1991 and involves the National Organization for Rivers and American Outdoors. Over 300,000 volunteers participated nationally in last year's cleanup effort.

The ArtSpace Labyrinth

More than a spiral, less than a maze, labyrinths are meditative by intent. True, a spiral pattern would compress a similar walking distance into the same area, but due to its simple symmetry, it will not engage the mind to the same extent. A labyrinth's occasional U-turns require just enough low-level attention to clear the mind of intruding thoughts, whereas mazes engage more of the conscious mind in order to solve the puzzle of the path, limiting their meditative value.

The distinction between labyrinths and mazes is that the former has one entrance, which doubles as the exit, and no branching choices. The path goes to the center and returns. Mazes have multiple branching choices, so there are always "right" and "wrong" ways to go. Typically, labyrinth borders are low to the ground or even painted on a floor. The center is visible from the entrance and from all points within the labyrinth. Walking across the lines is always an option. In contrast, mazes can be waist-high hedges, head-topping cornfields or even the claustrophobic trees in the movies *The Shining* or *Harry Potter and the Goblet of Fire*.

Whence labyrinths? Crete's myth placed the Minotaur at the center of what was more likely a maze than a labyrinth. Hopi Indians incorporated labyrinths into woven basket patterns. Walking medieval labyrinths, famously Chartres Cathedral, symbolized Pilgrims' progress to the Holy Land. Northern European peoples built hundreds of labyrinths, called "Troy Towns" on stony shorelines. In Finland, these were also referred to as "Jatulintarha," which translates as "Giant's Yard."

Maynard's publicly accessible labyrinth is part of the front lawn of ArtSpace, at 63 Summer Street. Lisa Bailey, artist and landscape architect, proposed, designed and, with volunteer help, constructed this project in 2007. It uses a Classic design, which can also be called a Cretan (after Crete) or seven-path design. Bailey visited other labyrinths before constructing this one, including those at Grace Cathedral in San Francisco. Her project involved spray-painting the lines, digging trenches, filling trench bottoms with stone dust and then setting granite blocks, weighing five to twenty pounds, in the stone dust. The entire effort took about one month. Financial support for the project came from the Maynard Cultural Council, Maynard Community Gardeners, ArtSpace and ArtSpace artists and individual contributions. For the numerically curious, this labyrinth is 28 by 32 feet across, and the border contains 536 granite blocks. It contains approximately 3.5 tons of stone and more

Lisa Bailey took a moment from her project to run upstairs into the ArtSpace building and take a picture of some of her volunteer labor force at work. *Photo by Lisa Bailey.*

than 4.0 tons of stone dust. Edge to center, a straight line, is less than 15 feet; following the path is 310 feet.

Bailey notes that "there is no right or wrong way to walk the labyrinth path…you may want to reflect on where you are in your life…or simply let your thoughts go and quiet your mind. When you reach the center, take some time to reflect, if you wish. The labyrinth is a metaphor for the journey of life."

Massachusetts has more than sixty labyrinths registered at www.labyrinthlocator.com or the Labyrinth Guild of New England at http://www.labyrinthguild.org. These include indoor, outdoor, church, public and private. For many, the registries include photos, directions and a contact person. The guild's calendar lists events, and it is also possible to rent labyrinths painted on canvas for your own event. Temporary labyrinths can be stomped into the snow or shaped in damp sand at low tide. World Labyrinth Day is the first Saturday in May.

Maynard Community Gardeners

Maplebrook Park sits on land that was originally part of a railway bed. In 1992, the lot was a blighted, weed-filled area that was slated to become a paved parking lot for the expanding Maynard Mall. A group of 35 concerned citizens attended a Planning Board meeting to protest this proposed use. The board asked for other proposals. Tresa Jones, Diane Russo and Felicia Reynolds, residents of Maple Street, said to each other, "We can make a garden." So they brought a proposal to the Planning Board for the installation of Maplebrook Park. At the next town meeting the proposal for the garden was approved by the citizens of Maynard along with an allocation of $2,000.

Thus begins a description of the origins of Maplebrook Park, at the corner of Summer and Maple Streets. The description is posted on the Maynard Community Gardeners (MCG) website, the founding of which in 1995 was a consequence of the park project.

Several historic horse-watering troughs scattered about Maynard serve as planters for the Maynard Community Gardeners. This one is at the intersection of Acton and Concord Streets. The Haynes family operated a construction supplies business.

The original volunteer group who helped plan and install Maplebrook Park included Tresa and Craig Jones, Lauren Tetreault, Russ Levine, Karen and Patrick Dunn, Diane and John Russo, Felicia Reynolds, Jack Whelan, Bobbie Statkus and many others. Department of Public Works staff including Walter Solokowski, Tim Hayes, Tim Mullally, Paul Anderson and Lou Mula helped clear the area and plant the trees and shrubs purchased with the town grant.

Since then, the Maynard Community Gardeners has grown to over one hundred members and is responsible for maintaining the park, the "Welcome to Maynard" planters at the town's entrance roads, plants in the historic horse-watering troughs in front of the fire station and elsewhere, such as the half-barrel planters throughout downtown, and the annual plant sale held each May.

Garden club types tend to split between talkers and doers. Talkers attend lectures by experts and then go home to tell their gardeners what is wanted. The clichéd answer from such a gardener, when asked what exactly she does in her garden, is to say, "I point." In contrast, MCG members are doers. Members put in weekend time at Maplebrook Park or take on personal responsibility for one or more of the half-barrel planters downtown. MCG was instrumental in getting the Maynard Community Farmers' Market started, as well as the annual town cleanups now managed by the Maynard Litter League. Looking forward, the group hopes to establish a Maynard community garden with plots for individuals to use for growing vegetables or flowers.

This is not to say that the Maynard Community Gardeners members are not also talkers and listeners. All year, but especially during the nongrowing season, MCG brings in speakers, holds social events and finds workshop for members to attend. In February 2011, members went to the Tower Hill Botanic Gardens in Boylston to see the Camellia Show, the Orangerie and the newly opened Limonaia garden.

The fifteenth-anniversary party of the Maynard Community Gardeners, in 2010, was a great example of creative and "green" spirit. Rather than a costly catered event for sixty members, the party was organized as an afternoon BYOT, as in "bring your own teacup." Each person was asked to bring their own tea cup, dessert plate, napkin and silverware. Subgroups were asked to bring teapots, desserts, folding tables, tablecloths, chairs and floral arrangements. The whole event magically set up, took place and cleared out in the course of a short afternoon.

The spring plant sale is a big fundraiser for MCG. It simultaneously allows members and nonmembers to share plants they are dividing or removing

The teapot table at the fifteenth anniversary of the founding of the Maynard Community Gardeners. Tresa Jones, MCG founder and one-time selectman for Maynard, spoke about MCG's history.

from their own gardens with others and raises money to help keep dues low and fund the year's events. The MCG mission is: "Dedicated to sharing a common interest in horticultural activities, promoting town beautification, and creating gardening opportunities for all."

Farmers' Market

"You people come into the market—the Greenmarket, in the open air under the downpouring sun." So begins "Giving Good Weight," first published in 1978 in *New Yorker* magazine, a story of farmers selling their produce in the greenmarkets of New York City as told by famed journalist John McPhee after he traveled the path from upstate dirt to downtown market. McPhee can be a bit wordy—thirty books and counting—but he nailed the economics and personal dynamics of small farms and face-to-face selling twenty-seven years before "locavore" became part of the green movement vocabulary.

Somewhere in the middle of that twenty-seven-year timeline is the beginning of the Maynard Community Farmers' Market. The summer of 1996 saw Anita Clemens and Daniel McCarthy push for the start of a farmers' market in Maynard. The concept started small but grew over the years. Sellers pay a weekly fee for booth space.

The location is the Clock Tower Place parking lot between Main Street and the mill pond. Summer Saturdays find some twenty to twenty-five booths selling everything from arugula to zucchini. Applefield Farm is a perennial, as is Balance Rock Dairy. Both of these operations also have stores open all week at their home sites.

Halfway down the row is ORG central: tables occupied by some of the various nonprofit organizations active in Maynard. The list includes Friends of the Assabet River Wildlife Refuge, Organization for the Assabet, Sudbury and Concord Rivers and so on. For those new to Maynard, this is a good means of learning what volunteer organizations exist and what they have to offer.

According to McPhee, "Giving good weight" is the opposite of the thumb on the scale. It embodies good will in concrete form: not only are we not cheating you, we are throwing in a bit extra. Back in the days of mechanical scales this practice was easier. You ask for a pound, the vendor throws a bit more than a pound on the scale, you pay the pound price. Today, with the electronic scale automatically calculating price, the "good weight" is less tangible but still there. It's the concept of the buyer supporting local farms in return for promise of fresher produce. Every successful merchant understands that the path to repeat business is delivering a bit more than you charge for.

The season usually runs from the last Saturday in June through first Saturday in October, 9:00 a.m. to 1:00 p.m., rain or shine.

According to its website:

> *The Market's mission is to provide area residents the opportunity to buy Massachusetts grown and produced products and support local farmers and specialty vendors. The Market also offers educational and cultural events, information about local nonprofit groups, and place to visit with friends and neighbors.*

Wildlife Refuge

Hunting is allowed in our neighboring wildlife refuge. The Massachusetts deer hunting season runs from mid-October to the end of December every day except Sundays. It is limited to bows, shotguns and muzzle-loading rifles. These are all short-range weapons compared to hunting rifles, lowering the risk of accidental shootings. The Assabet River National Wildlife Refuge also has hunting seasons for turkeys, grouse, woodcock, rabbits and squirrels. Deer hunters must wear orange. In season, so should you.

Origins of the refuge date back to the 1942 seizure of land spanning Maynard, Sudbury, Hudson and Stow by federal eminent domain. Landowners were given ten days to pack up and leave, and they received by their accounts around ten cents on the dollar of what the land was actually worth.

One of the most interesting features of the refuge is the World War II–era ammunition bunkers. The site was chosen to be convenient to railroad

Bunker 303 was on tour during the official opening of the Assabet River National Wildlife Refuge Visitors Center in October 2010.

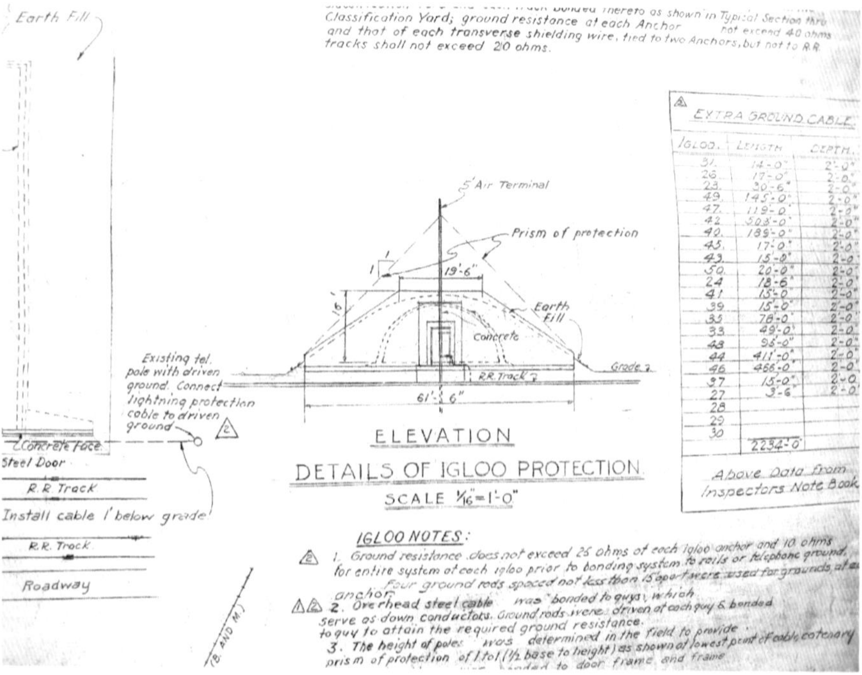

This blueprint of an ammunition bunker shows how much earth was heaped atop the inner concrete shell. The bunkers were spaced so that if one exploded it would not set off the others.

shipping to the Boston Navy Yard (1801–1974; current home to the USS *Constitution*), yet far enough inland so that a German battleship could not shell the area. Each of the fifty bunkers, officially referred to as "igloos," has inside dimensions of eighty-one by twenty-six by twelve feet and has a curved roof. Sides and roofs were mounded with dirt for extra protection and disguise. Today, from all but the door end, these bunkers resemble small hills, complete with a forest of trees growing on top. Bunker 303 is sometimes open for tours.

After World War II, this site, referred to as the Fort Devens-Sudbury Training Annex, served as a troop training ground, ordnance testing and laboratory disposal area for Natick Labs (U.S. Army Soldier Systems Center). A 1980s assessment led to this being categorized as an EPA "Superfund" cleanup site in 1990, as the site was contaminated with arsenic, pesticides and other chemicals. Extensive army cleanup efforts continued for years, ending with the site being turned over to the U.S. Fish & Wildlife Service in 2000 to turn it into a wildlife refuge.

The refuge covers 3.5 square miles. The prime purpose is to manage land for migratory bird conservation. A website (www.farnwr.org) maintained by Friends of the Assabet River National Wildlife Refuge has maps, photos, activities and a link to the government's refuge website. There is a wonderfully informative, child-friendly visitor's center at 680 Hudson Road, Sudbury. For people who just want to park and roam, the north parking lot is accessed from White Pond Road, reachable from Route 117 in Stow. Within the refuge there are 15.0 miles of old roads and new walking trails, with the old roads, which are in poor repair, open to bicycles. No pets are allowed anywhere in the refuge, along with horses, fires, overnight camping, ATVs, dirt bikes or snowmobiles. As of 2011, use of the refuge is free, but that may change.

Back to deer hunting: this is an example of a need to manage native species acting like an invasive species. Unrestricted hunting through the 1800s resulted in the New England extinction of wolves and mountain lions and near extinction of white-tailed deer. But with restrictions on hunting and the return of farmland to wilderness, the state deer population is roughly 100,000, or 10 per square mile, and much higher in favorable terrain. Without population management of some sort, deer destroy ecological balance. ARNWR allows deer hunting so it will be a refuge for all wildlife, not just deer.

One male, eighty-five-pound gray wolf made his way from Canada to western Massachusetts in 2007. Unfortunately he took up sheep killing rather than deer hunting and was shot. If more wolves emigrate from Canada, then the refuge will become a more interesting place to walk, as wolves hunt year-round, including Sundays.

Bibliography

Books

Allport, Susan. *Sermons in Stone: The Stone Walls of New England and New York.* New York: W.W. Norton & Company, 1990.

Boothroyd, Paul, and Lewis Halprin. *Assabet Mills: Images of America.* Mount Pleasant, SC: Arcadia Publishing, 1999.

———. *Maynard, Massachusetts: Images of America.* Mount Pleasant, SC: Arcadia Publishing, 1999.

———. *Maynard: Postcard History Series.* Mount Pleasant, SC: Arcadia Publishing, 2005.

Brown, Peggy Jo. *Hometown Soldiers: Civil War Veterans of Assabet Village and Maynard, Massachusetts.* Maynard, MA: Flying Heron Press, 2005.

Cummings, O.R. *Concord, Maynard & Hudson Street Railway.* Warehouse Point, CT: National Railway Historical Society, 1967.

Fuller, Ralph N. *Stow Things.* Stow, MA: Stow Historical Society, 2009.

Gutteridge, William H. *A Brief History of the Town of Maynard, Massachusetts.* Maynard, MA: Town of Maynard, 1921.

Hager, Lucie Caroline. *Boxborough: A New England Town and Its People.* Philadelphia, PA: J.W. Lewis & Co., 1891.

Halprin, Lewis, and Barbara Sipler. *Stow: Images of America.* Mount Pleasant, SC: Arcadia Publishing, 1999.

Heinrich, Bernd. *Summer World: A Season of Bounty*, New York: HarperCollins, 2009.

———. *Winter World: The Ingenuity of Animal Survival.* New York: HarperCollins, 2009.

Karr, Ronald Dale. *Lost Railroads of New England.* 2nd ed. Pepperell, MA: Branch Line Press, 1989

Lemire, Elise. *Black Walden.* Philadelphia, PA: University of Pennsylvania Press, 2009.

Nordskog, Michael. *The Opposite of Cold: The Northwoods Finnish Sauna Tradition.* Minneapolis: University of Minneapolis Press, 2010.

Seaburg, Carl, and Stanley Paterson. *The Ice King: Frederic Tudor and His Circle.* Boston: Massachusetts Historical Society, 2003.

Sheridan, Ralph. *A History of Maynard, 1871–1971.* Town of Maynard Historical Committee, 1971.

Stern, Philip. *The Annotated Walden.* New York: Barnes & Noble, 1970.

Thorson, Robert M. *Stone by Stone: The Magnificent History of New England's Stone Walls.* New York: Walker and Company, 2002

Voogd, Jan. *Maynard, Massachusetts: A House in the Village.* Charleston, SC: The History Press, 2007.

Weightman, Gavin. *The Frozen Water Trade.* New York: Hyperion Press, 2003.

WEBSITES

American Lyme Disease Foundation, www.aldf.com.

Assabet River Rail Trail, www.arrtinc.org/.

Birdsource: Birding with a Purpose, www.birdsource.org.

Boston Public Library. "Norman B. Leventhal Map Center." maps.bpl.org.

Boxborough Historical Society, www.multimgmt.com/BHSociety/bhs1.htm.

City-Data.com, www.city-data.com.

Eastern Coyote/Coywolf Research, http://www.easterncoyoteresearch.com.

Friends of the Assabet River National Wildlife Refuge, www.farnwr.org.

Historic Glass Bottle Identification & Information Website, www.sha.org/bottle/.

Internet Archive Digital, www.archive.org/.

Labyrinth Guild of New England, www.labyrinthguild.org.

Massachusetts Historical Society, www.masshist.org/.

Mass Audubon, www.massaudubon.org.

Maynard Community Farmers' Market, web.maynard.ma.us/civic/farmers/.

Maynard Community Gardeners, www.maynardgardeners.org/mcg/.

Maynard Historical Society, maynardhistory.org/.

Maynard Public Library, sites.google.com/site/maynardpubliclibrary/.
Organization for the Assabet, Sudbury and Concord Rivers, www.oars3rivers.org/.
Pilgrim Ship Lists Early 1600's, www.packrat-pro.com/ships/shiplist.htm.
Save Our Swans, www.savethemuteswans.com.
Stow Historical Society, stowhistoricalsociety.org/.
Sudbury Historical Society, www.sudbury01776.org/.
Tower Hill Botanic Gardens, www.towerhillbg.org.
U.S. Fish and Wildlife Service. "Assabet River National Wildlife Refuge." www.fws.gov/northeast/assabetriver/.
U.S. Geological Service. "USGS National Water Information System: Web Interface." waterdata.usgs.gov/usa/nwis/uv?01097000.
U.S. Historical Archive, www.ushistoricalarchive.com.
What Poison Ivy Looks Like, www.poison-ivy.org.

About the Author

Photo by John O'Buck.

David A. Mark lives in Maynard with his wife, Jean D'Amico, in their circa 1870 house. This is the eighth place in which they've lived together, and hopefully, it will become the longest period of time in one place—eleven years and counting. They have a barn that once had one horse stall and a chicken coop, the former now home for David's bicycles, the latter Jean's pottery studio. When not writing, Mark is a science consultant. When not writing or consulting, Mark enjoys gardening and bicycling. Most of the content of this book was written as a "Life Outdoors" column for the *Beacon-Villager* newspaper serving Maynard and Stow. Columns published subsequent to this book can be viewed at www.maynardlifeoutdoors.com.